ALIEN PARASITES

ALIEN PARASITES

40 GNOSTIC TRUTHS TO DEFEAT THE ARCHON INVASION

LAURENCE GALIAN

Alien Parasites: 40 Gnostic Truths to Defeat the Archon Invasion

Copyright © 2019 by Laurence Galian

All rights reserved.

Without limiting the rights under copyright reserved above, no part of this publication may be reproduced, stored in or introduced into a retrieval system, or transmitted, in any form, or by any means (electronic, mechanical, photocopying, recording, or otherwise), without the prior written permission of the author of this book.

The scanning, uploading and distribution of this book via the Internet or via any other means without the permission of the author is illegal and punishable by law. Please purchase only authorized electronic editions, and do not participate in or encourage electronic piracy of copyrighted materials.

While the author has made every effort to provide accurate Internet addresses at the time of publication, neither the author or his estate assumes any responsibility for errors or for changes that occur after publication. Further, the author and his estate does not assume any responsibility for author or third-party websites or their content.

If you believe that your copyrighted work is being infringed in this book, please notify the author, Laurence Galian, by electronic mail at this address: hong55431@mypacks.net who is the designated agent to receive notification of alleged copyright infringement, in accordance with 17 U.S.C. 512(c). Proper notification must include the following elements: (i) a physical or electronic signature of a person authorized to act on behalf of the owner of an exclusive right that is allegedly infringed; (ii) identification of the copyrighted work claimed to have been infringed, or, if multiple copyrighted works at a single online site are covered by a single notification, a representative list of such works at that site; (iii) identification of the material that is claimed to be infringing or to be the subject of infringing activity and that is to be removed or access to which is to be disabled, and information reasonably sufficient to permit the author to locate the material; (iv) information reasonably sufficient to permit the author to contact you, such as an address, telephone number and, if available, an electronic mail address at which you may be contacted; (v) a statement that you have a good faith belief that use of the material in the manner complained of is not authorized by the copyright owner, its agent, or the law; and (vi) a statement that the information in the notification is accurate and under penalty of perjury, that you are authorized to act on behalf of the owner of an exclusive right that is allegedly infringed. The author will act with all due diligence to remedy the problem as quickly as possible.

Editor: Eneida Flores

Illustration of Demiurge: Asterion Mage

Illustration of Sophia: Austin Osman Spare

Illustration of Nag Hammadi Codices: Shawn and Christopher Becker

Illustration of The Next Step: Aloria Weaver

Comments on the content of this book are welcome at:

gloggs37831@mypacks.net

ISBN: 9781099142765

CONTENTS

PREFACE 1
INTRODUCTION 6

PART ONE: THE PROBLEM 10

   KNOW YOUR ENEMY 11
   FIRST READ HERE BEFORE READING "THE SOLUTION" 12
   THE CHRISTOS AND UNCLEAN SPIRITS 14
   IDENTIFICATION OF THE ALIEN PARASITE IN YOURSELF AND OTHERS 15
   HOW DO THE ALIEN PARASITES BEGIN THEIR ATTACKS ON HUMANITY? 16
   GNOSTICISM 18
   WHAT DOES THE TERM "ALIEN PARASITES" MEAN? 20
   HOW DO ALIEN PARASITES CONTROL THEIR HOSTS? 25
   THE BATTLEFIELD 27

AN EXPLANATION OF THE GNOSTIC GALAXY 28

   THE PLEROMA 29
   THE AEONS 33
   CHRISTOS 35
   JESUS OF NAZARET 37
   SOPHIA 38
   THE ARCHONS 41
   THE DEMIURGE 43
   THE FULLY ACTUALIZED HUMAN BEING 52

QUINTESSENTIAL SUBSTANCE...53
GNOSTICISM: THE TEACHING BASED ON GNOSIS............55
METAPHYSICS...57
WHAT DID THE CHURCH DO ABOUT THESE REVELATIONS? 58
MORE ABOUT THE GNOSTICS 59
IS GNOSTICISM NEW? 63
THE GNOSTIC UNIVERSE AND VIRTUAL REALITY 65
IN THE BEGINNING WAS THE WORD 72
THE NAG HAMMADI LIBRARY AND THE ROMAN CATHOLIC CHURCH 74
WHAT GOSPEL IS THE TRUE GOSPEL? 83
HOW DID THIS HAPPEN? 85
THERE THEY WILL BE CALLED "CHILDREN OF THE LIVING GOD" 88
RESURRECTION 91
YOU ARE THE PLEROMA 93
WHAT IS REAL? 94
HAVE NO FEAR 101
DREAMS ARE THE WORLDS YOU CREATE 105
THE ROLE OF WOMEN IN GNOSTICISM 110
WHAT HAPPENED TO "THE DIVINE FEMININE"? 113
HOW TO PROTECT YOURSELF FROM THE ARCHONS 118
ALIEN PARASITES AND HUMANITY'S CHILDREN 120
MORE DETAILS ABOUT THE ARCHONS 121
HOW DOES A PERSON ATTRACT ALIEN PARASITES? 123

WHO ARE SOME OF THE MOST FAMOUS GNOSTICS? 124
BEWARE OF TEACHERS OF GNOSTICISM WHO MAKE
OUTRAGEOUS CLAIMS ABOUT THEMSELVES 131
GNOSTIC CONFESSION? 132
SIGNS THAT SOMEONE IS INFECTED WITH ALIEN
PARASITES 134
THE SECRET COSMIC BACK DOOR 135
HUMANS HAVE CREATIVE POWER 138
PARANOIA AND DELUSION 139
DIFFICULTY IN STUDYING GNOSTIC TEXTS 141

PART TWO: THE SOLUTION 145

ONE: PROTECTIVE SHIELD 146
TWO: STRENGTHEN YOUR MIND 148
THREE: NYMPHION 150
FOUR: SOUND REINFORCEMENT AND MOTIVATION 164
FIVE: PRAYERS 170
SIX: AFFIRMATIONS 172
SEVEN: NATURE 174
EIGHT: AROMA 175
NINE: SELF-OBSERVATION 176
TEN: THE DIVINE FACE 180
  A SPECIAL NOTE ON THE GNOSTIC TEACHINGS OF
  THE CRUCIFIXION 182
ELEVEN: POSITIVE FRAME OF MIND 189
TWELVE: PURIFICATION 191
THIRTEEN: THE POWER OF FLOWERS AND CACTI 193

FOURTEEN: INDIGENOUS RITUALS 194

FIFTEEN: CORRECT YOUR MISTAKES 195

SIXTEEN: UNLIMITED IMAGINATION 197

SEVENTEEN: SOLAR BREATHING 207

EIGHTEEN: ACADEMIA, SCHOLARS AND SCIENTISM 209

NINETEEN: AVOID NEGATIVE INFORMATION 221

TWENTY: DANGEROUS SPIRITUAL PATHS AND

SPIRITUAL LEADERS 224

TWENTY-ONE: DEPRESSING TALK 225

TWENTY-TWO: LIGHT OF THE SPIRITUAL WORLD 227

TWENTY-THREE: NEGATIVE ENERGY 229

TWENTY-FOUR: INTONE DIVINE NAMES 231

TWENTY-FIVE: USE AUTHENTIC ITEMS 233

TWENTY-SIX: ABSORB NEGATIVE ENERGIES 235

TWENTY-SEVEN: A WHITE CANDLE 238

TWENTY-EIGHT: BE GENEROUS 240

TWENTY-NINE: REORIENT YOURSELF 243

THIRTY: ADORE THE GODDESS 245

THIRTY-ONE: AVOID PLACES OF VICE (SLIPPERY PLACES) ... 247

THIRTY-TWO: BREAK YOUR ROUTINE 251

THIRTY-THREE: DEVELOP YOUR POTENTIAL

(PART A) 253

THIRTY-THREE: DEVELOP YOUR POTENTIAL

(PART B) 258

THIRTY-FOUR: REST 261

THIRTY-FIVE: MYSTICISM 263

THIRTY-SIX: PRAYER OF ENCOURAGEMENT 265

THIRTY-SEVEN: LIVE IN HARMONY 267

THIRTY-EIGHT: AVOID THE EXTREMES 268

THIRTY-NINE: DISTRACTION 269

FORTY: YOUR SACRED BODY 272

BONUS CHAPTER: THE ARTS CAN SAVE YOUR LIFE 275

SECOND BONUS CHAPTER: REAL OR SPIRITUAL? 278

HOW TO DEFEAT THE ALIEN PARASITES 281

THE NEXT STEP 285

CONCLUSION 287

APPENDIX 289

LAURENCE GALIAN BIOGRAPHY 292

LAURENCE GALIAN OTHER BOOKS 295

LAURENCE GALIAN WEBSITES 296

DISCLAIMER

The information included in this book is for educational purposes only and is not intended or implied to be a substitute for professional medical advice, diagnosis or treatment and does not constitute medical or other professional advice. Never disregard professional medical advice, or delay in seeking it, because of something you have read in this book. This is a spiritual book and the author is in no way suggesting that the reader avoid going to see an appropriate physician, medical doctor, or psychologist if he or she is suffering from physical and/or psychological symptoms.

In addition, the author declares that he has no connection whatsoever to Samael Aun Weor, any of the organizations that he founded, nor any offshoots from these organizations. Further, the author expressly asserts that he does not believe or follow any of the teachings, doctrines, tenets, creeds, nor ideologies of the above said man.

"Now, therefore, lift up your face, that you may receive the things that I shall teach you today and may tell them to your fellow spirits who are from the unwavering race of the perfect Human."

~ *Papyrus Berolinensis Gnosticus*

PREFACE

The author wants to make it absolutely clear that this is a work of non-fiction whose creator, in good faith, assumes responsibility for the truth or accuracy of the events, people and information presented. This is a book written for the general public. It is not a textbook. The author does not present technical vocabulary, without a clear explanation of the word or words being used. The majority of books written about Gnosticism are written by university professors or by people who have obtained a graduate level academic or professional degree in the subject. There exists a formal or artificial form of communicating prevalent in institutes of higher education. This style of academic writing is called "academese."

This author wants the book you are now reading to be very informative but not dry, pretentious or weighed down by technical jargon. The primary purpose of this book is to educate the everyday person about Alien Parasites and how to defeat them using the wisdom of Gnosticism. Therefore, you do not need a university degree in order to understand and identify with the contents of this book.

While researchers, academicians and professors are invited to read this book, the author does not use the style or language of academic scholarship. Nor does this book obey rules of academic writing. For example, every university student is forbidden to use the phrase "*There is* . . ." when they are writing a thesis or dissertation because university rules state that this expression has no meaning. This is laughable as *The New King James Version* of the Bible contains the phrase "*There is* . . ." 1130 times! This does not include the thousands of other academic writing "errors" that the *New King James Version* of the Bible contains. In addition, academics say that it is prohibited to use the second-person pronoun "you," and that the author must use formal language.

The author is writing this book for you, my good friend, family member, neighbor, paralegal, automotive technician, dentist, gardener, construction worker, hairdresser, plumber, music teacher, electrician, DJ, web developer, coach, small business owner, maintenance and repair worker, nurse, in short, whoever is concerned about alien mind parasites, whether or not you completed high school, or have a doctorate in theology. If you have common sense, this book that you are now reading will be helpful for you.

Humanity is under attack and this is not the time to warn only those people who are capable of writing a doctoral thesis, rather it is time to alert each and every person to this threat to humanity.

Mircea Eliade (March 8, 1907 - April 22, 1986) was a Romanian historian of religion, fiction writer, philosopher and professor at the University of Chicago. Eliade was one of the most influential scholars of religion of the 20th century and one of the world's foremost interpreters of religious symbolism and myth. He wrote:

A religious phenomenon will only be recognized as such if it is grasped at its own level, that is to say, if it is studied as something religious. To try to grasp the essence of such phenomenon by means of physiology, psychology, sociology, economics, linguistics, art or any other study is false; it misses the one unique and irreducible element in it - the element of the sacred.

The author is sounding the alarm that humanity is under invasion. The attack is spiritual in nature, as you will discover through the reading this book. Certain forces are seeking to replace all of humanity's spiritual impulses, with impulses designed to sink humanity ever deeper into scientific materialism. Humanity is gradually becoming enmeshed in technology.

Along with the gradual disappearance of true and profound spirituality, these evil forces want to fill humanity with false illusions and egotism. Human beings under the control of Alien Parasites display attraction to superficial matters such as: titles, award ceremonies, rank, knowledge for knowledge sake and so on. Humanity must rise above the temptations of egoic titles, obsessive study and the pursuit of an endless amount of university degrees and certificates of study.

During the coming years, there will be a great focus on science, to the exclusion of all other opinions about reality. Science and technology are good and helpful pursuits, but science is only one aspect of reality. Those who worship at the altar of Scientism, are only viewing one part of the whole. Megan E. Holstein former tech founder, published with Apress and located at meganeholstein.com writes the following about how human culture is in great danger of misunderstanding the definition of learning, as well as of intelligence and the ability of schools to assess the students' very worth!

Because schools only teach and assess the ability to memorize, students have no opportunity to exercise their intelligence outside of this. According to schools, the only way a student can be smart is if they can memorize well. Because this is how schools judge students, students learn to judge each other on this as well. They begin ranking their intelligence (and even their worth) by their ability to memorize.

Surprisingly, part of the attack which humanity is undergoing, is the flow of a concept into people's minds that true spirituality is something that brings with it warm, relaxed and good feelings. The beings attacking humanity want human beings to believe in the simple, easy going perusal of the Gospels, an approach beloved by most religious denominations and sects today. At the same time (it must be remembered that the enemy is sophisticated), another part of humanity is being encouraged by these evil beings to believe in a literal reading and interpretation of the Bible. This orthodox approach is just as dangerous as a completely atheistic and materialistic view of the world.

Transhumanism and the rise of cyborgs will increasingly move humanity from a profound and direct experience with the Divine. Science and academic research are very important for humanity's growth and evolution as human beings on this planet. The danger lies in the overly sentimental and simple-minded concepts of religion and spirituality that are popular themes in today's spiritual books. True spirituality is something that is as complex, and at the same time subtle, as the most advanced study of particle physics. A person must devote many years of study, meditation, prayer and other spiritual disciplines, in order to properly develop himself or herself spiritually. Humanity, at this time, must let go of the illusion that true spirituality consists of a kind of emotional "high," or on the other hand, that true spirituality consists of a kind of militaristic, fanatically disciplined obedience to a vast list of rules and regulations.

INTRODUCTION

Do you know Alien Parasites could be attacking you at this very moment? Do you wake up in the morning angry over nothing? You don't have any good reason to be angry, but you still wake up in a bad mood. Do you get angry with the way your breakfast is prepared or served? Do you get angry with other drivers on the road, or the way someone looks at you while you're getting on the subway or the bus to work? During the day, do you get angry with your boss and co-workers? It seems like the anger and rage inside you is just growing and growing. And then, in the evening, you watch the news and become even more infuriated. Why? Alien Parasites. Are you jealous and out of control? Are you ashamed of yourself and full of guilt? Maybe you walk around all day sad and depressed? You cry at the drop of a hat. Or maybe you feel envious of your neighbor? Do you suffer from overwhelming depression, anxiety, panic attacks and suicidal thoughts? Are you experiencing powerful negative emotions and images that you don't normally have? Are you experiencing strong odors of unknown origin that manifest spontaneously and disappear just as quickly? Why? Alien Parasites. These beings literally feed off your negative energy: anger, guilt, jealousy, depression, frustration, sadness and fear; for these intense and often harmful emotions are a gourmet dinner for these evil beings.

What about your thoughts? Are they your own thoughts? Have you ever wondered why you suddenly have an impulse to jump out of a window or a cliff? Do you sometimes have to fight a strong impulse to say something horribly cruel and completely unprovoked to someone close to you?

This book will teach you how to identify if you are under a parasitic attack by Alien Parasites and how to remove these parasites from your mind.

One afternoon, a local farmer named Muhammed al-Samman and his brother were digging around some caves in Egypt. The year was 1945 and they were near Quenoboskion, a village 6 miles from the modern city of Nag Hammadi. The two were looking for fertilizer. Both brothers also knew that sometimes these caves yielded up objects worth selling in town. Suddenly, clunk! Their shovel struck an object. Upon clearing the dirt and debris away from the thing, they realized it was a very large earthenware jar. "Well," they thought, "maybe it contains something of value." So, they carried it back to their home. When they arrived home, they opened the large jar and to their great disappointment discovered that it only contained a repository of old books. "Probably worthless," they thought, "but maybe one of the rich people in town will want to buy one." So, they didn't throw the books in the garbage, but it seems that they forgot about the old jar.

Pervading every corner of the Middle-East, is an ever-present fear of evil beings, nonhuman invisible beings, call *Jinn*. Somehow, Hollywood caught hold of this idea of powerful Jinn (that could grant wishes if they were friendly) and they renamed them "genies," and they appeared in many films about exotic Arabian Nights. However, the Jinn's true reality was not so charming. The Jinn were once worshipped by pre-Islamic Arabs, so great was their power. However, and of great importance to this book, they are believed to be able to cause disease, mental illnesses and possess people. Thus, the mother of the two brothers, became very suspicious of this old earthenware jar and decided that it might contain Jinn. She subsequently began to burn the books. Fortunately, the brothers discovered what she was doing and were able to save most of the books. The brothers became involved in a feud, and decided to leave the manuscripts with a Coptic priest. In October of 1946, a brother-in-law of one of the two men, sold a book to the Coptic Museum in Old Cairo. Thus, began a long "Indiana Jones" saga during which finally the books found their way to scholars who could translate them and who realized their value. The contents of the books in that humble jar are changing the world. Yes, they were old books. Very old. About 2,000 years old. And what did they contain? The most incredible treasure in the world — gospels and epistles written about Jesus Christ — and the authors were none other than the Apostles and others disciples close to Jesus Christ! They tell a very different story than the one that has come down to the human race via the four gospels of the New Testament. This collection of leather-bound papyrus books are now called "The Nag Hammadi Library" or "The Nag Hammadi Codices." They contain information about various groups of deeply spiritual followers of Jesus of whom historians and experts in early Christianity had little knowledge. Collectively, these groups were named the Gnostics.

PART ONE: THE PROBLEM

KNOW YOUR ENEMY

Many of you have felt or intuited that these Alien Parasites exist. Many of you have felt that most of humanity lives in slavery. Some of you may be aware, through reading various books or through direct experience, that a parasite lives inside your mind. My task is to convince those of you who doubt the existence of Alien Parasites that they do exist. And for those who think or know that they exist, my task is to free you and protect you from them! In any battle, it is essential to "know your enemy." Unless you want to underestimate the danger these Alien Parasites pose, unless you want to live life as a slave, unless you want your soul eaten away completely, this author recommends you read the following description of exactly what is going on in this universe.

FIRST READ HERE BEFORE READING "THE SOLUTION"

First, let me tell you that you are welcome to go to the second part of this book entitled "The Solution" if you feel that you are under attack by Alien Parasites and the situation has risen to the level of an emergency. However, this author advises you that you will find several terms that are unfamiliar to you in the second part of the book. Therefore, if you feel that you must immediately go to the "The Solution" section, by all means do so, but then come back here so that you can fully understand the terms and thus strengthen your defenses against Alien Parasites.

A lot of people don't know they have Alien Parasites. Alien Parasites project themselves into human beings, live virtually in the skull (in some cases other parts of the body) and treat people as transport vehicles as they themselves are not physically allowed on Planet Earth. Alien Parasites attack the human mind by "Implantation of Ideas". Then, they insert into the human host various thoughts like:

Your life is nothing but an illusion. I've created reality for you. Your past never existed. All your past memories are implants.

They make their victims (usually referred to as "hosts") think the whole world is a kind of lie, a simulation. People finally become nothing more than empty shells, the walking dead, in service to these Alien Parasites.

THE CHRISTOS AND UNCLEAN SPIRITS

The Christos (from the Greek, meaning "anointed") spent a lot of His time, while on Earth, healing people. This author is specifically referring to the fact that the Christos spent a lot of time casting out what the Bible calls unclean spirits. These unclean spirits are Alien Parasites. Mark's Gospel is replete with examples of this aspect of the Christos' healing ministry. In Christianity, there is talk about good angels and evil angels; in Islam, the pious and evil jinn, in Buddhism and other religions, beneficent spirits and malevolent spirits. Alien Parasites have been attacking humanity since humans first walked on this Planet.

IDENTIFICATION OF THE ALIEN PARASITE IN YOURSELF AND OTHERS

It is almost impossible for a person with an advanced condition of alien parasitic intrusion to recognize that they are under the control of the parasite. However, if your case is not too advanced, here are several ways you can realize that your mind has been invaded by an Alien Parasite: feelings of insignificance, meaninglessness, lack of emotion, indifference, feelings of dissociation, overwhelmed with irrational fears, passionate hatred of people from another country, race, religion or culture, desire to kill or "see killed" people from another nation and so on, feeling that you are going crazy, feeling self-righteous, unable to control your tongue and finding yourself saying horrible things to people. Some examples of severe alien attack are: the belief that you are a rock or an inanimate object, that your dog is controlling you, that a famous pop singer or Hollywood star is in love with you, the belief that God is punishing you for your "sins" by (for example) causing your boyfriend to die in a car accident, or the belief that the news anchor is speaking directly to you from television.

HOW DO THE ALIEN PARASITES BEGIN THEIR ATTACKS ON HUMANITY?

They begin by invading the minds of individuals in government, military, medicine, finance, media, education, academia, secret societies and religion. They give these individuals what is essentially a computer virus. From these foxholes, they launch their spiritual warfare against the general population and against specific individuals. Often people who are reading about Alien Parasites do not understand how they can invade the Earth when they are not even allowed to physically be present on the planet. Yet, these same people do not wonder how Wi-Fi can bring an ultra-high-definition (UHD) image of the president giving a speech into their smart phones or how satellites can send images of the planet Mars back to Earth! Those individuals who study science know that through *quantum entanglement* it is possible to send "entangled" encryption keys from a satellite to an Earth-based receiving station. The NASA Deep Space Network (DSN) is an international network of antennas that provide the communication links between the scientists and engineers on Earth to the Mars Exploration Rovers during their flights in space and while they are on Mars. Astronauts regularly beam their voices and images into the headsets and screens of their mission handlers who are here on Earth. Finally, the Frey Effect enables scientists to send speech directly inside the human head without any kind of radio receiver implanted inside the person. In the *Walter Reed Army Institute of Research*, United States Army scientists, using "voice modulated microwaves" were able to demonstrate that they could project words directly to a specific person's brain. Without getting overly technical, it is easy to see how Alien Parasites can project themselves into the skulls of specific human beings.

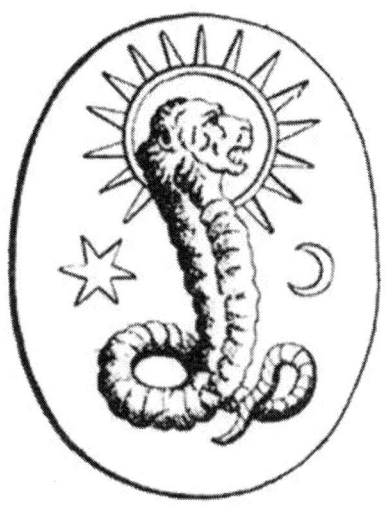

GNOSTICISM

To understand these Alien Parasites, where they come from and what their intentions are, the reader must explore the teachings of Gnosticism. The Gnostics are a group of wise adepts who understand the mysteries and secrets of the universe. To truly understand Gnosticism, one must travel far back in time, before the time of Christ Jesus, even before the first Egyptians, all the way back to the very foundations of the world. Here, in the very bedrocks of the world, can one begin to understand Gnosis.

The term "Gnostic" comes from the Greek: *Gnosis*. Gnosis is direct spiritual knowledge. The Gnostics are the seers, initiates and shamans among humanity. The Gnostic can make contact, through Gnosis, with the One True Reality.

Gnosticism is the best description of why the Planet Earth exists, and why there is life on this Earth. Gnosticism is the best explanation for the origin of humanity, extraterrestrial visitors, national and international politics and shadow governments. Gnosticism is a complete explanation of how life works in this world, galaxy and universe, in addition to what is happening in other dimensions, parallel universes, and simulations.

Gnosticism is for the pure of heart. Henri-Charles Puech, (July 20, 1902 - January 11, 1986) was a French historian who long held the chair of History of religions at the Collège de France from 1952 to 1972. Puech himself wrote this definition of Gnosis:

The Gnosis is an inner experience through which a human being during an illumination which is at the same time regeneration and deification takes control of his truth again and regains consciousness of himself, in other words, of his state of being and his origin. In this way, he acknowledges or recognizes himself in God and appears to himself as stemming from God and as a stranger in this world.

WHAT DOES THE TERM "ALIEN PARASITES" MEAN?

Alien Parasites are what the Gnostics call "Archons." They cause delusions in people's thinking because they convince their victims to believe things that are not true. A delusional person has false or unrealistic beliefs or opinions. A delusional person is someone who has a belief that is held with an extremely strong conviction despite superior evidence to the contrary. Now, this trait may be a brave attribute, but the delusional person refuses to listen and consider the opposite opinion. The mature and wise individual always is willing to listen to an opposing opinion, and actually is eager to hear the opposing point of view, in order to make sure his or her theories and beliefs can withstand all opposing ideas and to revise his or her ideas if necessary.

Gnostics call these Archons "parasites" because they, in essence, live inside the minds of human beings. They steal psychic and life energy from human beings as they slowly devour their hosts. They're aliens because they're not indigenous to this planet. Archons existed before there were human beings on this planet. Alien Parasites serve people lies and install false realities while they are feeding off these people. Almost everyone has experienced nightmares, and some people have experienced a type of dream far worse and far more dramatic, called a "night terror." These dreams can be extremely vivid and terrifying for a while, but as soon as the person wakes up, he or she realizes that the night terror was just a dream. What makes dreams so fascinating to this discussion is that when a person is dreaming, he or she believes that the dream is real. When the person wakes up, he or she realizes that the dream was only a subconscious simulation that tricked him or her into believing it was real. The pounding heart and sweating brow of the person who just had a nightmare attests to how real the nightmare was for him or her during their dream experience. This demonstrates at a simple level, that you can and do believe in reality simulations generated by your own mind, at least while you are asleep. This leads to the inescapable conclusion that you are vulnerable to other types of reality simulations. Of course, everything you experience – everything, whether you call it normal waking consciousness, deep sleep, meditation, or drug-induced perceptions – is real. However, some realities lack an integral congruence; they lack an alignment with the attributes of the nature of the Absolute. When people say, "Something smells rotten," they are intuitively referring to the fact that something is not in harmony with the truth or it is synthetic (lacking in authenticity).

The Archons are also said to be aliens because for those with clairvoyant sight, Archons physically resemble many of the popular images the public has of extraterrestrials: small bodies, large heads, enormously large eyes; sometimes appearing fishlike or reptilian. In the Gnostic text on the *Origin of the World* it is affirmed that the Archons are like an aborted fetus since they do not have spirit. In the (First) *Apocalypse of James*, the Christos calls the Archons:

alien beings

Jay Weidner, famous filmmaker, author and scholar, on Rense Radio stated the following about the Archons:

Gnostics preached that there was an invasion that occurred about 3,600 BC and, about 1,600 years before the Nag Hammadi texts were buried, they wrote that this invasion was like a virus and, in fact, they were hard pressed to describe it. The beings that were invading were called Archons. These Archons had the ability to duplicate reality, to fool us. They were jealous of us because we have an essence of some kind, a soul, that they don't possess and the Nag Hammadi texts describe the Archons. One looks like a reptile and the other looks like an unformed baby or a fetus. It is partially living and partially non-living and has grey skin and dark, unmoving eyes. The Archons are duplicating reality so that when we buy into it, when we come to believe that the duplicated, false state reality is the real reality – then they become the victors.

Paul Chen, journalist for *The Canadian* newspaper, adds the following information:

By understanding what it means to be human, according to ancient Gnostics, Manipulative Extraterrestrials became revealed. Manipulative Extraterrestrials seek to confuse a critical appreciation among human beings, of their 'essence' as intelligent sentient beings. However, if one can appreciate the 'essence' of what it means to be human, Manipulative Extraterrestrials are revealed by "subtracting" that essence, from an 'alien shadow' that seeks to occupy the same time-space with the human essence. The "alien shadow" can be compared to a parasitic virus, which latches on to healthy cells in a body, in a manner that debilitates those healthy cells toward their prospective destruction. Gnostics detected Manipulative Extraterrestrials that they called 'Archons' as an artificial intelligence that pursues an agenda of pure ego…

There are millions of alien races and many of them help humanity on a regular basis. However, there is a group of aliens (the Archons) who are invading this planet, not through direct military force, but through an invasion of the human mind. They are aliens, make no mistake. However, they are not physically allowed on Planet Earth. In the movie *Constantine* someone says to the lead character, John Constantine, an exorcist:

We're finger puppets to them, John, not doorways. They can work us, but they can't come through onto our plane.

Beneficial aliens also function through consciousness, since the battle with the Alien Parasites takes place in your consciousness through *holographic simulation*. Virtuous alien races are actively helping you in this war.

HOW DO ALIEN PARASITES CONTROL THEIR HOSTS?

The Archons use "mind control" techniques. This is known as psychological warfare, but Archontic manipulation far surpasses anything the United States, Russia, Vatican City, Israel, or the United Kingdom has, as of yet, invented. The Archons are the ultimate brainwashers. The Archons keep people distracted with pornography and drugs, with sports and alcohol, with material possessions, exotic vacations, artificial reality, addiction to various pleasures, along with dreams of the artificial technological paradise of radical life-extension, transhumanism, nootropics and Brain Computer Interfaces. The Archons do this so that humanity does not have the time or opportunity to observe what is really happening in the world. Humanity is under siege. The Archons want you to be as uneducated and uninformed as possible. They destroy your passion for learning, and infiltrate and sabotage the educational system. Ultimately, they want to destroy all that makes you human, your hopes, your dreams, your joys, especially they want to destroy your spirituality. The Archons don't want you to be concerned about other people; they want you to obsess over your physical appearance and your bank account. In *the Gospel According to Mary Magdalene*, the Christos says,

"This is why you get sick and die; because you love what deceives you. Anyone who thinks should consider these matters!"

THE BATTLEFIELD

Do you suspect that someone you know, your wife, husband, relative, friend, co-worker, is being attacked by the Archons? As somebody concerned about Alien Parasites, you will need to understand Gnosticism in more detail. When you understand the specifics, you'll have a kind of map that will help you to understand the battlefield. Make no mistake, you're in a battle with beings that want to destroy every last shred of your humanity. Through carefully reading the description that follows, you will begin to understand exactly who the enemy is, who your allies are, where God is in all of this and exactly how Alien Parasites enter a person's body.

AN EXPLANATION OF THE GNOSTIC GALAXY

THE PLEROMA

The *Pleroma* plays a central role in Gnostic cosmology. The Pleroma has a physical location in the astronomical mythology of Gnosticism; it is situated in the center of the Milky Way galaxy. Another way of saying this is that the Pleroma is found in the Human Heart (*As above, so below*). The Pleroma is called: The Fullness, The Totality of the Divine Powers, The Galactic Nucleus, The Divine Fullness of Life, The Perfect Whole, The Absolute Causality, Kingdom of Light, The Original House, the House of Perfection, The Gardens of Light, The Spontaneity, The Region of Light, The Living Plasma, The Place of Eternal Ideas or Archetypes, The Electromagnetic Consciousness and The Energetic Field.

According to the Gnostic Adepts, in the beginning existed an Ocean of Bright Light. This Light shone with great intensity. This Shining Light was (and continues to be) emanated by the Ultimate Reality. Gnostics do not directly name this Absolute Reality. The Gnostic book entitled *The Gospel of the Egyptians* says that the Ultimate Reality is the:

. . . *unrevealable, unmarked, ageless, unproclaimable Father*

He is described as "*the great invisible Spirit*" which is "*the silence of silent silence*".

In the *Sophia of Jesus Christ*, Matthew asks Jesus:

> *Teach us the truth.*

to which Jesus replies:

> *He Who Is, is ineffable. He is unnamable. He is ever incomprehensible.*

The Supreme Reality, also known as the Uncreated or the First Being, manifested its own fullness. For reasons which will become increasingly clear, Gnostics have always been reserved when it comes to naming this Absolute Reality. Another way of looking at the Supreme Reality is that there is a Reality behind everyday reality. Miguel Conner, the great contemporary Gnostic, calls this Reality,

> *The God above god.*

Gnostics want humanity to know that there is a God behind the traditional god of religions. Another way of putting this concept is to state that there is a sun at midnight. In this regard, Omraam Mikhaël Aïvanhov, the illustrious Bulgarian philosopher, pedagogue, mystic and esotericist, wrote:

Beyond the visible sun is the invisible, 'dark Sun' which pours a ceaseless stream of energies into our visible sun and the visible sun transforms them and sends them on in the form of light. The dark sun emitted the primordial Light which the visible sun transforms and sends out as rays of visible light.

In the ancient Sufi oral tradition, Divine Reality says:

I was a Hidden Treasure and then I desired to be known so I created a creation to which I made Myself known; then they knew Me.

Inside the Pleroma, dwells the Uncreated One (the First Being, the Reality, the Mighty Splendor), as well as what one might call *revelatory expressions of dynamism*, or Gods and Goddesses. Nikola Tesla, one of the greatest geniuses in the history of science, described the process of the Uncreated One emanating the Gods and Goddesses of the Pleroma as:

The primary substance, thrown into infinitesimal whirls of prodigious velocity.

These fountains of outpouring energy are called the *Aeons*. The Pleroma is overflowing with love. Another way of looking at the Pleroma is that there is a Reality behind everyday reality. The Pleroma sought to know its own depth.

Nikola Tesla spoke about the Pleroma which he named the "core":

My brain is only a receiver, in the universe there is a core from which we obtain knowledge, strength and inspiration.

And he divulged that in the core:

Everything is spinning, everything is moving, everywhere there is energy.

It is important to mention that the *Maya* believed, along with the Gnostics, that the center of the galaxy was a place of great spiritual significance. The greatest expression of divinity for the Maya living in the Yucatan peninsula was *Hunab Ku* (the highest authority). Hunab Ku lives in the center of the galaxy. Hunab Ku is represented by the spiral. This spiral form can be found throughout Mesoamerica.

THE AEONS

In the Galactic Nucleus, in the place known as the Pleroma, are located a group of glorious beings named the *Aeons*. They are emanations of the Absolute Reality. They may also be considered divisions within the Godhead, as well as the various aspects or dimensions of the Infinitely Pre-Existent and in some spiritual traditions, the Names of God. The Aeons always exist in pairs, a masculine and feminine principle; in other words, each Aeon has its own consort. They may travel from the Pleroma. Among the Aeons is the Feminine Expression of Divinity - Sophia - and her Divine Consort - the Christos.

Do not imagine the Aeons in a human form, for they are whirling energy vortices. Some Gnostics speak of them in terms of numbers and sounds. They bear a great resemblance to angels and exist as beings of Light. In fact, according to certain Gnostic schools, angels such as Armozel, are also Aeons. They design life-forms (for more information on this practice, consult the works of Rudolf Joseph Laurence Steiner). Their spiritual purpose in originating genetic life-forms is for the purpose of uttering an infinity of Divine Expressions. The Aeons created the Human Genome.

Ancient and modern psychonauts (people who use natural psychedelic plants and mushrooms for spiritual purposes) have known about the Aeons for thousands of years. The author has personally experienced the Aeons and Archons firsthand. John Lamb Lash, a leading exponent of the power of myth to direct individual experience, describes the Aeons as plasma filaments that fill the universe. These filaments consist of spores, for example, fungal spores or seeds. Together, with the Absolute Source from which they emanate, the Aeons form the Pleroma, or The Divine Fullness of Life, and therefore should not be considered as distinct from the Divine One, but as symbolic abstractions of the divine nature.

CHRISTOS

Christos means "the anointed one." The name is derived from the Greek word *Christós*. This was a name applied to Jesus by the first Greek-speaking Christians. It is a translation of the Hebrew word *mashiyach*, commonly written in English "Messiah," which also means "anointed" and usually refers to a consecrated person (for example: a king, priest, or saint); specifically, the Messiah.

However, to the Gnostics, the Christos is an Aeon, dwelling in the Pleroma. The Christos is the *syzygy* (male Aeonic consort) of Sophia. In this book, a distinction is drawn between the Christos and Jesus. When the book is referring to the time before the baptism by John the Baptist, he is referred to as: Jesus. After the baptism, the book uses the term "Christos." In addition, this book refers to Him as the Christos, rather than the more common term "Christ" to remind the reader that the Christos is a separate being in and of Himself, and not just, as the popular saying goes "the second name of Jesus." When the Christos incarnated in the man Jesus, He united Himself with the destiny of the Planet Earth.

The Christos is the perfect beauty and star of the Pleroma. Through the Hermetic principle of "As above, so below," the Christos first was revealed as the *Solar Logos* (the Spiritual Sun), the deity that governs the entire solar system, of which the Sun is the most external manifestation. Consider that, without proper training, the average person cannot look directly into the sunlight. The fact that the sun is so bright is evidence that it is the material manifestation of a great spiritual being. Madame Helena Petrovna Blavatsky revealed that there is one:

Central Spiritual Sun, whose beams and effulgence are only mirrored by our central Star, the Sun.

The Sun is the source of all life on Earth. This concept of the Solar Logos has been adopted by many ancient teachings such as those of Hermes Trismegistus and other Gnostic Adepts. The Christos is the spiritual sun, the source of enlightenment that brings about order, harmony, spiritual insight and the awakening of the divine potential within each human being. Rudolf Steiner stated, that the Christ is:

the Spirit Who from the beginning has come down to us from the Sun.

Christos, the sperm, now dwells in the center of Sophia, the Earth, the fertilized ovum.

JESUS OF NAZARET

It's a man's name. His full name was "Yeshua ben Yosef" (Jesus son of Joseph). According to *Strong's Concordance* "Nazaret" is a valid transliteration of the word Ναζαρέτ, ἡ. Jesus was an Initiated Adept. However, he was not born as the Christos. Jesus was prepared by Sophia, through many Earthly incarnations, to become a pure vessel for the reception of the Christos. According to Valentinus, a Gnostic adept of the second century, the Christos is:

> *the Paraclete (Helper) from the Unknown who reveals . . . the discovery of self – the divine spark within you.*

The Christos descended upon Jesus, and remained in him, beginning at his Baptism. Jesus represents a conscious unification with the Source. Occasionally, this book uses the phrase "Christ Jesus" when speaking about the historical life of this amazing being, when referring to titles of certain books from the *Nag Hammadi Library* and to call to mind the wonderful event that took place when a human being so prepared himself that he became transformed into an Aeonic Avatar of Love streaming from the Pleroma.

SOPHIA

Sophia, Mother of the Universe, whom some call Love.

Eugnostos the Blessed

Sophia is an Aeon. Sophia is how energy takes form. Her soul and the world are one. Sophia is the Great Mother Goddess known by countless names throughout the millennia. Some people think She is the Holy Spirit of the Trinity (The Gnostic *Gospel of the Egyptians* speaks of *"the father, the mother and the Son"*). Today, She is often referred to as Gaia or Mother Earth. Her consort in the Pleroma is the Christos. She is the Bride of the Christos.

Sophia left the Galactic Nucleus (The Pleroma), because she had a creative vision of intelligent living human beings (mirror images of the Aeons). Sophia was so fascinated by her dream of a new type of Aeon with a complete organic body (containing all the elements: earth, air, fire and water) that with a sudden passionate impulse she jumped into one of the arms of the Milky Way *without* the company of her balanced male consort, the Christos. In doing so, there was an unexpected incident. This was an unparalleled and unheard-of event. Because of Her "fall" from the Pleroma, an extraordinary event occurred. Ever since Sophia designed the Earth and ever since she fell in love with her imagination of organic images of the Aeons, she shared her consciousness with her creation. She completed the human being, for a human being is composed not only of earth, air, fire and water, but also of spirit. She gave Her all for a glorious dream. However, Sophia's amorous leap from the heights of the Pleroma, Her leap into the unknown, had unforeseen consequences. The force of Her energetic leap of love was so powerful that when She came into contact with inorganic metallic matter, an astonishing catastrophe materialized. Along with Her intention to create humanity, the involuntary interaction with these unusual substances, created a kind of mechanical race of robotic beings that was a horrible imitation of humanity.

After sharing Her Living Being with the Earth, Sophia fell into a deep sleep, because she was separated from Her consort, the Christos. The job of humanity is to prepare themselves, as Jesus of Nazaret did, to receive the Christos. When the waters of the Light of Christos flow through you, and you become the Christos, Sophia recognizes you as Her consort and She awakens. She is the force that is continually working within you throughout your life that inspires you to rise to the Light, to receive the Christos.

Sophia resides in all of humanity as the hidden wisdom, and She is humankind's secret identity as indwellers of the Pleroma. Sophia is the highest ruler over the visible universe and at the same time, the mediator between the upper and lower kingdoms. She is the Mother of the Living. She is the "Unveiler of the Mysteries of the

Whole Magnitude." Sophia is an artist, making this visible underworld an image of the glorious Archetype. In the Gnostic book *Trimorphic Protennoia* found in the Nag Hammadi Library, you will discover these amazing words from Sophia:

"It is through me that Gnosis comes forth. I dwell in the ineffable and unknowable ones. I am perception and knowledge, uttering a Voice by means of thought. I am the real Voice. I cry out in everyone, and they recognize it (the voice) since a seed indwells them."

THE ARCHONS

When Sophia became one with her Creation, this was more than a simple unification, she became the physical planet along with the very beings who inhabit it. Planet Earth is a materialization of Sophia's body. The energy involved was enormous as it flowed directly from the Galactic Center! When the electromagnetic flow of Sophia's intention approached specific types of metaloids, fermions, subatomic particles, and ions, this contact formed creatures similar to cyborgs; insectoid creatures, called *Qlifot* (fragments of broken vessels) in the Lurian Kabbalah, or the Archons in Gnosticism. The Archons feed off of the dark emotions of human beings. They are energy vampires.

Archons live mainly in Saturn's Rings. Rome was known by the "Romans" as Saturnia, not as Rome; Saturn was one of the Roman gods. However, the Archons do not respect the limits of their living space, nor do they respect the limits of the purposes for which they were created.

Therefore, they meddle with human beings, inserting deviant thoughts into their minds. They are influence peddlers, a type of non-physical implant, a foreign installation in the brain, from which they launch their mind-control system.

They cannot physically enter the Planet Earth because the core of this Planet is now the abode of Sophia re-united with her consort, the Christos. When the Christos saw the distress of Sophia, He traveled from the Pleroma to help awaken Sophia from her nightmare and to help her in her struggle against the mechanical robotic imitations of humanity.

While the Archons cannot physically touchdown on Planet Earth, they can project their thoughts telepathically and their images holographically. They are experts in creating simulations of all kinds, inverting and distorting your perception and in this way, they create an Archontic Inversion. Archons are deceivers *par excellence*. They live in hive-like structures. They are more like robots than living beings, as they lack intentionality and imagination. In other words, they follow orders like an army of automatons.

Therefore, Archons manipulate people to create situations that are ideal for creating sources of food for themselves, situations such as war, terrorism, child sexual abuse, political confrontations, drug addiction, high taxation, low wages, the cult of the self, the dehumanization of worker, the immorality of the super-rich and so forth.

THE DEMIURGE

The "Son of Chaos". The *Demiurge* is the presumed "almighty" god of the Archons, who can only create copies of archetypal patterns that exist in the Pleroma (but he cannot instill the divine spark). *Yaldabaoth* is the name of the Demiurge. The Gnostic book entitled *The Apocryphon of John* states the following about the Demiurge:

Now the archon who is weak has three names. The first name is Yaldabaoth, the second is Saklas and the third is Samael. And he is impious in his arrogance which is in him, for he said, 'I am God and there is no other God beside me.'

There is a true God beyond the "god" of Judaism, Christianity and Islam. This "god" (who is the god of most of the world religions) in reality is the Demiurge, who insanely thinks he is the one true god. Most Gnostics teach that Yahweh (also known as Jehovah) of the Old Testament is none other than the Demiurge. The Gnostics gradually reached this conclusion by studying the writings of the Old Testament which demonstrate that Yahweh is a violent, jealous, mass murderer, a cruel and ruthless deity who indiscriminately orders the execution of innocent men, women and children or directly carries out their deaths by various means. Here are three examples:

Yahweh is a man of war. Yahweh is his name.

Exodus 15:3

I form the light and create darkness. I make peace and create calamity. I am Yahweh, who does all these things.

Isaiah 45:7

For Yahweh your God is a devouring fire, a jealous God.

Deuteronomy 4:24

On the other hand, Christos descended from the realm of Light and brought humanity the light of true knowledge in the simple principles of love. Marcion de Sinope (85 – 160 C.E.) was an important leader in early Christianity. Marcion, in his two brilliant books, explained how the God of the Jews was not the God of whom Jesus spoke. He provided many examples that show that the Jewish god is only a jealous tribal deity. The Old Testament contains some genuine wisdom. However, it is very clear that the Hebrew prophets and rabbis gradually destroyed all trace of the Divine Feminine (the Goddess) and worshipped the Demiurge. The same applies to the other main patriarchal religions: Islam and Christianity. There are always holy men and women (who are members of the patriarchal religions) who because of their pure and ecstatic love can travel beyond the Demiurge and the Archons and directly access the Pleroma. However, there have been very few individuals who have accomplished this great feat.

Each religion has an *exoteric* (public) side and an *esoteric* (secret) side. The secrets of how to contact the Divine directly are contained in the esoteric teachings of the world's major religions. For example, the *Kabbalah* contains the secret inner teaching of Judaism, *Sufism* contains the secret inner teaching of Islam, and *Rosicrucianism* contains the secret inner teaching of Christianity.

The Demiurge has his henchmen: called Archons, who insert strange thoughts into people's minds. The Demiurge wants total control of the Earth's planetary destiny and is the greatest threat to humanity.

All secrets are in Saturn,

declared Pythagoras, possibly implying that the Demiurge has made his home on Planet Saturn. Origen of Alexandria (185 CE — 254 CE), also known as Origen Adamantius ("man of steel"), was one of the earliest and most important Christian scholars. He stated plainly that Yadabaoth (one of the names of the Demiurge) was the Planet Saturn.

Some Gnostic texts appear to state that the Demiurge created the Earth, the home of humanity. Other Gnostic texts infer that this planet is a malformed copy, created by the Demiurge, of the true Earth. This information is useful, but the information must be explained in more detail. The Gnostic has always been free to express his or her Gnosis in the manner he or she wishes. The Gnostics of the Nag Hammadi Library perhaps could be considered free thought, free spirited seekers of Gnosis, who rejected authority and dogma. Thus, as the Christos regularly taught through parable, so too the Gnostic adepts taught through story and myth. What then were these Gnostic Initiates writing about when they speak about the Demiurge's connection to the Earth? It is important to define the terms being used here, and first understand what an Initiate is and what he or she is not. An "Initiate" is someone who has "crossed the boundary (or threshold)." The greatest Initiates have crossed the boundary of death and have returned — they have been called the *twice born*, the *born again*, or those *born from above*. These Initiates are often referred to as the Enlightened. However, the spiritual voyage consists of many steps, and thus in reality there are many initiations that the seeker experiences on the path to knowing the Divine. Each initiation is the badge of having overcome some challenge or barrier. The greatest work consists of developing a knowledge of oneself. This is not a "conquest" of the self, but rather a kind of comprehension of one's entire self, or one might say the art of creating a working integration of all the aspects of one's self. The Initiate has harnessed or "mastered" the various subtle bodies every human being possesses (such as knowing and integrating one's emotions, and knowing and integrating the mind, rather than being at the mercy of emotions and thoughts). The Initiate is like a wise leader who has brought all of his or her society into a state of harmony. The Christos told us:

The kingdom is inside of you, and outside of you.

Gospel of Thomas

What he was referring to is the fact that there are two worlds: the true glory of Sophia and the false world of the Demiurge. The false world of the Demiurge seems the same as the world of Sophia, except that it is, to use a metaphor, colorless. The world of the Demiurge is the world as it seems to people obsessed with material possessions, attracted by the desire to control the realm of the Goddess Sophia, people who prefer the artificial to the authentic, people in the clutches of delusional poisonous drugs, people with addictions to other people and alcohol, as well as food, spending, pornography, gambling, angry people who are fixated with politics and financial issues; people who are full of illusory worries about possible future events rather than living in the authentic present now, people who see the world through the eyes of the media and people who are completely isolated from themselves emotionally. These people never "see" and never "hear" the real world around and within them. They live in the false duplicate reality of the Earth manufactured by Yaldabaoth. This facsimile is an illusory world;

A poor and fragile copy of the Eternal Kingdom,

as the great contemporary Gnostic, Miguel Conner, describes it. In short, Yaldabaoth's world is a world without love. This false Earth is a cold, frightful, violent, two-dimensional world. This is the *Matrix* of the movie of the same name. When a person opens his or her heart to love, he or she is instantly transported to the Real Earth. Suddenly, Sophia's world unfolds before the person, a world of color, depth, joy and deep meaning. During an interview with the cutting-edge Belgian website *Karmapolis*, John Lamb Lash offered the following insightful words of wisdom:

The Archons influence the way you perceive the world, not the world itself. The primary power in the world we inhabit is the indwelling divinity of the planet, the Gaian intelligence, called Sophia by the Gnostics. If you are aligned to the Gaian intelligence, you do not see the world as a place of fear and predation, but of beauty, bounty and magic.

It is important to note that the imitation of Yaldabaoth's Earth is a thought in his mind. Yaldabaoth's Earth is not real. The point for the reader to remember is that when a person feels and thinks that the world, in which he or she is living, is a horrible and loveless place, he or she has entered Yaldabaoth's mind.

Chris Hedges, author and host of RT America's "On Contact," recently joined Rick Sanchez on a show released on March 11, 2019 to discuss the skyrocketing problem of suicide and self-destructive behavior in the United States. A recent report from the CDC announced that deaths due to alcohol, drugs and suicide are higher than ever. The Demiurge is attacking humanity with a deep hatred, and humanity is in a fight for its very survival. It is obligatory for the student of Gnosticism to immediately practice the techniques given in this book in order to escape from the Demiurge's false vision of reality. He's the great deceiver and he wants you to think his world is the real world. Many people trapped in the Demiurge's imitation of the Earth think that they are realistic and practical, and that the people of love, the people of Gaia/Sophia, are desperately deceived. These trapped people take great pride in the fact that they think they are more sophisticated than people who follow a spiritual path. They believe that they are the ones who really understand reality, when in fact this is part of Yaldabaoth's deception; he caresses the egos of his followers telling them that they are special because they can know the facts about reality. However, these are not facts, these "facts" are just lies. The only "reality" they know is Yaldabaoth's false invention.

His methods of getting people into his artificial world are very attractive. He tells people that if they spend a lot of time listening and reading the daily news, getting involved in political parties and feeling indignant about the problems of the world, that somehow, they will change the world and make it a better world. The Demiurge always wants people to worry about the future. He doesn't want people to live in the present, in the now. He wants you to always be unhappy with the present and always thinking about the future. He wants you to complain constantly and feel dissatisfied. The Demiurge wants you to concentrate on what's wrong with people and things. He tells you that's the smart way to live your life. However, the way to change the world is through first loving the One Supreme Reality, secondly, loving yourself and thirdly, loving the people closest to you: your family, your neighbors and the people you work with every day.

There are many other beings that you will discover in the Gnostic Galaxy if you choose to delve more deeply into Gnosticism. For instance, there is Barbelo, who speaks of Herself in the *Trimorphic Protennoia*:

I move in every creature... I am the Invisible One within the All... It is I who poured forth the water. It is I who am hidden by radiant waters. It is I who gradually put forth the All by my Thought. It is I who am laden with the Voice. It is through me that Gnosis comes forth.

While She appears in certain Gnostic texts such as the *Three Steles of Seth* and the above *Trimorphic Protennoia*, Barbelo is a very complex being, often portrayed as androgynous. There are also such beings as: Adamas, Norea, Epinoia, Eve, Abrasax (or Abraxas), Seth, Autogenes, Youel, Acamoth, as well as many others. However, for the purposes of this book, which focuses on how to protect you from Alien Parasites, it is necessary to stop the description of all the wondrous beings you will encounter in the Gnostic cosmos, and for you now to begin to put the information already given to you into a useful purpose.

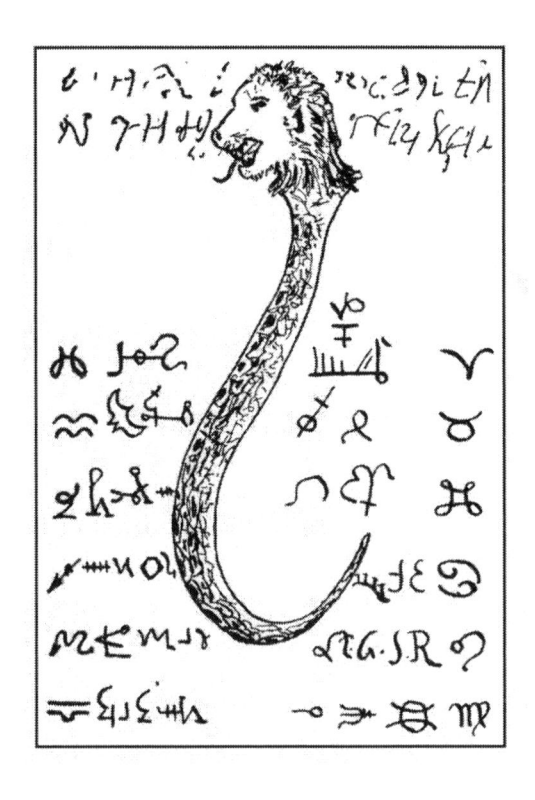

THE FULLY ACTUALIZED HUMAN BEING

The fully actualized human being is the christified human being.

. . . and put on the new man, who in the likeness of God has been created in righteousness and holiness of truth.

Ephesians 4:24

In the *Book of Thomas the Contender*, the Christos speaks secret words concerning self-knowledge:

For he who has not known himself has known nothing, but he who has known himself has at the same time already achieved knowledge about the depth of the all.

The fully actualized human being is a person who maximizes his or her potential. This activation process attempts to move consciousness from one reality to another, including the incorporation of being aware of multiple realities existing simultaneously. The objective of the actualized integral human being is to unite with the One, the Source, to achieve unity (from the Greek *henosis*) and to perfect oneself. A deep secret lies in the words of John Shelby Spong, a retired American bishop of the Episcopal Church. He said:

The way you become divine is to become fully human.

QUINTESSENTIAL SUBSTANCE

The One (the Uncreated or the First Being) is the high source of the Pleroma. The One is Infinite. Nicholas of Cusa was a Late Medieval author who made use of the ancient saying:

God is an infinite sphere, whose center is everywhere and whose circumference is nowhere.

Infinity is integral. Integral means whole, intact, undivided, full and unbroken. Infinity cannot be divided against itself. The One is also coherent. Coherent means clear, consistent, sonorous, intelligible. All Divine Reality is present in each and every point within itself. Ernest Holmes writes:

The whole of God is present in each and every point of God.

This spirit that dwells in each and every person also inhabits all existence. James Russell Lowell in his poem *The Vision of Sir Launfal* inscribed these words:

That thread of the all-sustaining Beauty

Which runs through all and doth all unite

There is a living presence dwelling in everything. The final substance from which all forms are created. The poet Charles Haddon Spurgeon wrote,

There is no place where God is not.

Stones, plants, animals and human beings are made of the same infinite substance. The author had the good fortune to meet Swami Dayananda. In one of his discourses, the Swami explained that there are many different types of jewelry that are made of gold, but while there are many gold rings, necklaces, bracelets and so forth, there is only one substance: gold. Gold has the capability (the inherent nature) to take on various forms. The Quintessence can take any shape. Intelligence guides the hands of the jeweler, as Intelligence guides the Creator. If something is shapeless and without form, only Intelligence operating through it can give it form.

The secret of the quintessence is found in the pentagram. The pentagram is a human glyph. The star on the staff has five points. Four of these points represent earth, air, fire and water. The fifth point is the quintessence that interpenetrates everything: the Spirit.

Paracelsus taught us:

We do not know the quintessence because we are fooling away our time with outward and perishing things, and are asleep in regard to that which is real within ourselves.

GNOSTICISM: THE TEACHING BASED ON GNOSIS

Gnosticism means "Direct Spiritual Knowing", being in direct experience with the Creative Source. Gnosticism has been called "forbidden self-discovery" by the Church, for it is a form of illumination. In other words, Gnosticism does not need the structure of a church to function. It is therefore, a threat to the existence of many denominations.

The Arab Gnostic Monomius declared:

Abandon the search for God and the creation and other matters of a similar sort. Look for him by taking yourself as the starting point. Learn who it is within you who makes everything his own and says, "My God, my mind, my thought, my soul, my body." Learn the sources of sorrow, joy, love, hate. Learn how it happens that one watches without willing, rests without willing, becomes angry without willing, loves without willing. If you carefully investigate these matters you will find him in yourself.

Many years later, in the 20th century, Ernest Holmes wrote:

All the power that there is and all the presence that there is, and all the life that there is, is God – the Living Spirit Almighty – and this Divine and Living Spirit is within me.

Clement of Alexander (Stromata 13,2;15,2) explains that there are teachings reserved for a few, and transmitted orally. He has this to say about these "mystery" teachings:

To James the Just, and John and Peter, the Lord after His resurrection imparted knowledge (τὴν γνῶσιν.) These imparted it to the rest of the apostles, and the rest of the apostles to the Seventy, of whom Barnabas was one.

METAPHYSICS

Metaphysics is the knowledge of that which is beyond the known laws of physics. Otherwise stated, metaphysics is information about things, forces and beings that scientists have not yet discovered or understood. *The Apocryphon of John* speaks about the indwelling spirit:

For he does not exist in something inferior to him, since everything exists in him.

Thus, no matter how far or near one travels, one can never find a place outside of Spirit.

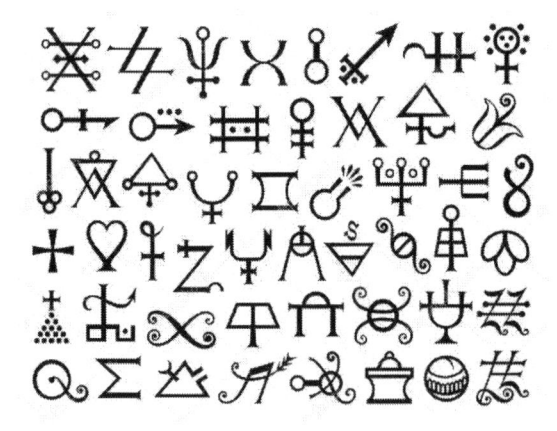

WHAT DID THE CHURCH DO ABOUT THESE REVELATIONS?

The Roman Catholic Church began to label the Gnostics as heretics starting around 200 CE and the Catholic Church today continues to do everything possible to ignore, repress and denigrate the Gnostic teachings. Little by little, the power-hungry men who made up the majority of the Roman Catholic Church leaders were able to destroy almost all of the original teachings of the Christos regarding how to encounter the Absolute Reality.

MORE ABOUT THE GNOSTICS

The wisdom of the *Gnostics* is called Gnosis. Gnosis cannot be understood through doctrine or dogma. The Gnostics believe that you can have a direct experience with the Infinite Spirit. Who is the Infinite Spirit? Many people wonder why this author does not just write the word "God." Millions of people have gone to churches, temples and other places of worship and have heard the pastor, reverend, or priest speaking about God. Unfortunately, many of these religious leaders, cannot express and explain adequately to the congregation, who God is. Often, these religious leaders themselves have childish notions about God. How do you describe the indescribable? Many religious leaders teach that God is an Old Man with a long beard, who demands that you obey all his laws and regulations. People's minds are filled with nonsense about God. Throughout your childhood all sorts of people tried to explain to you, "Who is God?" Eventually, you developed a collection of inadequate explanations of the Absolute Essence. Each human being has their own individual concept of God. People spend their lives filled with guilt, fear and worry about the punishments that this "God" is going to inflict on them after they die. Gnostics do not need faith because they are already having a direct relationship with the Absolute Essence. As an example, if you are riding a motorcycle, you do not need to have faith that you have a motorcycle in order to ride it, because it is supremely obvious.

For this reason, it may be helpful to you if for a while, you stop using this word "God," because your mind is filled with all sorts of confusing thoughts and beliefs about God. You need to clear your mind of all contradictory and imperfect concepts of who and what God is. Change your language and you change your thought. The Absolute is the One Being who gave rise to all of existence; this Being is the Radiance of Your Existence, the Living Presence of Life that is Fully Awake Within Itself, the Perfect, That Which is Beyond Any Intellectual Understanding.

You do not need to have faith that oxygen is in the air. You simply breathe normally. The oxygen is in you and around you. You cannot see it, but you can breathe it. You know it exists. You do not need faith in oxygen to breathe. In this exact way, you have a direct connection to Formless Divine Consciousness. This book will help you recognize and strengthen that connection, and realize that you do not need belief in God, because you will gradually come to know that the Absolute Reality is closer to you than the air you breathe.

St. Teresa of Avila, in the sixteenth century, gave specific directions to help people to find the Beloved:

This magnificent refuge is inside you. Enter. Shatter the darkness that shrouds the doorway. Be bold. Be humble. Put away the incense and forget the incantations they taught you. Ask no permission from the authorities. Close your eyes and follow your breath to the still place that leads to the invisible path that leads you home. Follow your breath.

Some people, for all intents and purposes, are "dead", because the Alien Parasites have completely taken them over. The Alien Parasites choose certain people to be their Generals in their warfare against humanity. These generals can be found in the world of advertising, politics, orthodox religion, military, medicine and the entertainment industry. However, the Alien Parasites are contented that, for the most part, they have dulled the minds of humanity to the point that most people are like cattle or sheep. The public thinks they are happy if they have a new car, the latest model television, plenty of beer, alcohol and drugs to consume. Those with a little more money buy yachts, mansions, designer and personally tailored clothes, custom made furniture, expensive grooming for their pets, costly paintings, nannies, collections of cars, private schools and living technology-infused lifestyles.

While the following is a bit stereotypical, it nevertheless contains more than a morsel of truth. The strategies Archons often use against men to dull their minds are: fast cars, washing and waxing their cars, non-stop football marathons, obsessions with baseball and basketball, betting on sports, fantasy sports, videogame obsessions, pornography, the latest high-tech gadgets, drinking vast quantities of beer, politics, and binge-watching a single television series. For women the Archons frequently attack through these methods: glamor, fashion magazines, department store sales, politics, nonstop shopping, plastic surgery, making unnecessary purchases of shoes, accessories and jewelry, as well as watching soap operas.

You may be ruled by greed without realizing it. Do not let it eradicate the nature of your story. Too often, people carry around so much pain in their hearts, that they surround their hearts with an impenetrable wall. In order to make up for the lack of love, people change their focus from their hearts to their brains. The limbic system of the brain likes to collect things and declare its territory. Sadly, because most people lack the courage to open up their hearts again (to possibly being hurt once again), they try to substitute physical assets for the lack of joy that can only be found in the heart. The Demiurge is very happy if you are living in your brain and you take pleasure in acquiring objects, rather than through the many varieties of love. Material possessions bring a kind of fleeting pleasure, but they will never provide a deep joy. Only love brings joy. And to love, one needs courage.

IS GNOSTICISM NEW?

Gnosticism has been in existence for a very long time, back to the very origins of humanity. Gnosticism is simply the knowledge of the hidden and mysterious wisdom of what lies behind the world. It has had several names over time, but it has always existed. At one time, it was known as *The Eleusinian Mysteries* or simply *The Mysteries*. People who practiced Gnosticism were happy and fulfilled and had no fear of death. They knew they were Divine beings who could not die. Human beings are vibratory energetic beings. Energy can't die. By the time when the great Initiate Jesus was born, Gnosticism was already a well-developed spiritual practice.

There were many Gnostic adepts and several "schools" of Gnostic thought and practice. Therefore, there exist variations in the Gnostic teachings. However, this is the beauty of Gnosticism. Gnostics are not bound by a Catechism or a Bible. Gnosticism is ultimately your relationship to the Divine and no one has the right to tell you that your personal experience is right or wrong.

None of the various Gnostic groups that existed approximately during the first and second century of the Common Era (*anno Domini* or AD), which scholars today term Gnostic groups, called themselves by that name. Gnosticism is a seventeenth-century term that scholars invented to define those groups that sought truth and direct experience with the Divine, and who existed approximately during the first two hundred years after the Christos walked the Earth in a physical body. Gnosticism is the acquisition of divine knowledge through deep meditation and ecstatic revelation. Gnosticism is the purest and most direct way of knowing the Divine and the Universe. The word Gnosis was used by the Greeks for "knowledge" - not everyday common knowledge, but deep knowledge that can only be gained through direct individual revelation. In other words, it is "Divine Knowledge".

THE GNOSTIC UNIVERSE AND VIRTUAL REALITY

The Gnostic Universe is divided into levels, realms and what some call hierarchies. Interestingly, in recent years, some of the world's most renowned physicists have declared that humanity is living in a computer simulation. Many famous recent films also depict humans living in a matrix or in an "artificial world". In February 2000, a new and very unusual computer game was created. Even the word "game" is not an adequate word to describe this computer program. The name of this program is now world famous. This program has no defined objectives. The player creates individual "people" and places them in houses and helps to direct their moods and satisfy their desires. The player can control the daily activities of these virtual "humans".

By March 2002 this game had sold more than eleven point three million copies, making it the best-selling personal computer game in history. The characters in this game advance through six stages of life, from infancy to old age and subsequent death. Each character exhibits wants and fears according to their aspiration and personality. Throughout the ensuing years, this game has continued to develop in sophistication and complexity. New elements have been added: personality development (the "people" may have desires and goals that they pursue in gradual steps as humans do in "real" life), specific days of the week, vacation days for adults and weekends for children during which they can relax and play at home.

The characters in this game can leave the house and visit other locations, also they can obtain job promotions and so forth. In the most recent version of the game, the "reality" that the characters live, takes place in real time and real time is needed to complete an action. In other words, in most other video games, movies and television shows, the program can skip ahead several hours, days and even years while you are watching the video game or show. A film can represent an individual's entire life. However, with the new version of this computer game, the player must spend the exact amount of time that his or her character spends, for example, waiting in the doctor's waiting room. In addition, players can now progress through fifty-five levels, create up to thirty-five characters, create town maps, construct buildings, plant, bake, marry, have pets and even have a baby!

This computer game is the best-selling game of all time, with the original version selling sixteen million units. Thus, when scientists and other great thinkers of modern times say that humanity lives in a Virtual Reality Universe, it is obvious that, if humanity can create a world like this best-selling computer game that people can run on their personal home computers, an extraterrestrial civilization a thousand years more advanced than the human race, could easily create a computer game that would be indistinguishable from what humans now call everyday reality. With the amazing advances the world has seen in the computer "video-gaming" world during the last fifty years, there are no limits to the degrees of development and sophistication that the future computer programmers will attain.

Leading scientists and philosophers such as Nick Bostrom, contend that if an advanced civilization created us, most probably this "advanced civilization" is also a creation of an even more advanced civilization. And that this "even more advanced civilization" is also the result of an *even more advanced civilization*. This almost endless repetition must still have an ultimate programmer. Some scientists are saying that for some reason an advanced race of aliens might create such a computer game in order to see how their very remote ancestors (ancestors who may have lived thousands of years ago) lived and evolved. This is called an "ancestor simulation". Perhaps a very advanced race of aliens no longer needs physical bodies. A being from such an advanced race of aliens may want to create an "ancestor simulation" program to experience what life was like when they had physical bodies, made love, felt physical pleasure, pain and had to work for a living.

The creation of artificial realities is not much different from how people enjoy today's movies depicting life in ancient Egypt, life during the Middle Ages, depiction of various wars, or life during the Renaissance. Humanity is living in a virtual reality universe, a video game created by a civilization 1,000 to 100,000 years older than the human race. And they themselves are also simulations (virtual reality). These levels of hierarchies can extend to a vast degree above us, creating levels of gods or spirits.

There are the *lower* level gods and goddesses, who dwell in the lower astral realm, such as those found in belief systems such as Santeria, Vodun, Palo Mayombe (or Palo Mallombe), Santa Muerte, Candomblé, Esú or Eshú (in Yoruba language "sphere"), Kimbanda and Ifa. There are also intermediate spirits such as saints, angels and archangels; and a still higher being called by various names such as: Yahweh, El and Allah, who is the Demiurge. The programmers of this simulation also created demons and fallen angels.

Because there are many levels in this gigantic video game, people pray to the beings on the lower and intermediate levels, as they are often easier to contact than the more exalted beings (for example, these lower and intermediate beings often respond to human and animal blood sacrifice, offerings of large amounts of gold or money, flagellation, fasting and other offerings of material goods such as flowers, food and incense. The public hopes that, by petitioning the beings on the intermediate level (saints, angels and archangels), their request will be transmitted to the Supreme Reality (the ultimate controller of the game). In other words, in reality people are asking the intermediate level of programmers to change the program. When people pray for a miracle, they are really praying that the computer code of one of the levels will change to give them what they want. They are trying to contact and influence the intermediate programmers when they pray. Maybe the programmers are human beings, a million years into the future.

Some of you might be wondering:

How can intermediate level beings see or experience this artificial life? The answer is that people already have virtual reality goggles through which they can view, in three dimensions, sporting events on the opposite side of the world. Today you can purchase equipment that enables you to watch and listen to a professional basketball game that takes place in the United States while you are in your bedroom in Japan, wearing virtual reality goggles and headphones. Imagine the authenticity, accuracy and realism of virtual reality that a civilization a thousand years more advanced than humankind can produce! Currently, manufacturers of virtual reality products are working on new technologies that will make it impossible for your human senses to detect any difference between the reality you experience in everyday life and the virtual reality you will experience when you use their products. These manufacturers are also working on gloves and other interfaces so that you can feel the virtual people and objects you touch.

The advanced, and probably for the most part benevolent aliens (intermediate programmers), are not creating computer games in the ordinary sense of the term. These games are more like works of art, improvisational theater, performance art, scientific and philosophic investigation and historical novels. They are works of love created by the intermediate beings that exist between this level of existence and the levels of excellence. The Supreme Beings in the Pleroma, the Aeons, act only from Pure Love.

Interestingly, the malicious Archons themselves are similar to this present day's current computer game characters, in the sense that they have a "sort" of life, the appearance of being real. A thread of quantum vibration traverses all revelations and appearances of reality in whatever form it may take. The supposed Spirit-Matter duality is based on a misunderstanding of the perception of the Essence. The body is nothing more than a coalesced soul. The soul is nothing more than the mystical body. The famous genius, physicist Niels Bohr, said:

Everything we call real is made of things that cannot be regarded as real.

IN THE BEGINNING WAS THE WORD

God is Infinite, and as a person partakes in this Infinite Reality, he or she is also partaking in the infinite variations of this Reality. There's no solid reality as people commonly think of it. All is vibration. Nikola Tesla is reported to have declared:

If you want to find the secrets of the universe, think in terms of energy, frequency and vibration.

John 1:1 announces:

In the beginning was the Word, and the Word was with God and the Word was God.

What is a word? It is a sound vibration! And what is the intelligence behind this vibration that "thinks" the Word? The answer is MIND (or what some call consciousness, intention or god). The Gnostic text called *The Apocryphon of John* affirms that the Unique Primary Reality:

. . . is pure, immeasurable mind.

In the Gnostic book *Trimorphic Protennoia*, the text states:

It is through me that Gnosis comes forth. I dwell in the ineffable and unknowable ones. I am perception and knowledge, uttering a Voice by means of thought. I am the real Voice. I cry out in everyone, and they recognize it (the voice), since a seed indwells them.

In short, there is a mind behind matter. Max Planck, the theoretical physicist who originated quantum theory, which won him the Nobel Prize in Physics in 1918, wrote:

I regard consciousness as fundamental. I regard matter as derivative from consciousness. We cannot get behind consciousness. Everything that we talk about, everything that we regard as existing, postulates consciousness.

God is PURE, ORIGINAL MIND.

Sir James Hopwood Jeans (September 11, 1877 - September 16, 1946) British physicist, astronomer and mathematician wrote:

...the stream of knowledge is heading towards a non-mechanical reality; the universe begins to look more like a great thought than like a great machine. Mind no longer appears as an accidental intruder into the realm of matter; we are beginning to suspect that we ought rather to hail it as a creator and governor of the realm of matter...

Our holy and sacred minds are part of the Divine Consciousness.

Psalms 82:6 proclaims:

> *I said, "You are gods, all of you are sons of the Most High.*

THE NAG HAMMADI LIBRARY AND THE ROMAN CATHOLIC CHURCH

What if there was something so controversial about the life of Jesus that the early Roman Catholic Church would not want to make this information available to the public? As the author has already explained, in 1945, a farmer in southern Egypt made a surprising discovery: he unearthed previously unknown Gospels, Apocalypses and Epistles that had been buried underground for nearly two thousand years. His discovery is known as the Nag Hammadi Library. The library is a collection of thirteen ancient books (also called "codices") and they contain more than fifty texts. Following is a list of these amazing books:

The Acts of Peter and the Twelve Apostles

Allogenes – The Foreigner

The Apocalypse (Revelation) of Adam

The (First) Apocalypse (Revelation) of James

The (Second) Apocalypse (Revelation) of James

The Apocalypse (Revelation) of Paul

The Apocalypse (Revelation) of Peter

The Apocryphon (Secret Book) of James

The Apocryphon (Secret Book) of John

Asclepius 21-29

Authoritative Teaching

The Book of Thomas the Contender

The Concept of Our Great Power

The Dialogue of the Savior

The Discourse on the Eighth and Ninth

Eugnostos the Blessed

The Exegesis on the Soul

The Gospel of the Egyptians

The Gospel of Philip

The Gospel of Thomas

The Gospel of Truth

The Hypostasis of the Archons – The Reality of the Rulers

Hypsiphrone

The Interpretation of Knowledge

The Letter of Peter to Philip

Marsanes

Melchizedek

On the Anointing

On the Baptism A

On the Baptism B

On the Eucharist A

On the Eucharist B

On the Origin of the World

The Paraphrase of Shem

Plato, Republic 588A-589B

The Prayer of the Apostle Paul

The Prayer of Thanksgiving

The Second Treatise of the Great Seth

The Sentences of Sextus

The Sophia of Jesus Christ

The Teachings of Silvanus

The Testimony of Truth

The Thought of Norea

The Three Steles of Seth

The Thunder, Perfect Mind

The Treatise on the Resurrection

Trimorphic Protennoia – Three Forms of First Thought

The Tripartite Tractate

A Valentinian Exposition

Zostrianos

Tragically, the Catholic Church destroyed an enormous amount of texts about which the public will never know. They are lost in the sands of time. However, other Gnostic texts have been recovered that may not have been included in the texts found at Nag Hammadi (as some of these precious codices were originally thought to be worthless and therefore used as kindling for cooking), but these other texts were found elsewhere. They come from non-Christian spiritual lineages. The Gnostic Society (2560 N. Beachwood Drive, Hollywood CA 90068) writes the following on their excellent website about Gnostic works that were not found at Nag Hammadi:

The Hermetic tradition represents a non-Christian lineage of Hellenistic Gnosticism. The tradition and its writings date to at least the first century B.C.E., and the texts we possess were all written prior to the second century C.E. The surviving writings of the tradition, known as the Corpus Hermeticum (the "Hermetic body of writings") were lost to the Latin West after classical times, but survived in eastern Byzantine libraries. Their rediscovery and translation into Latin during the late-fifteenth century by the Italian

Renaissance court of Cosimo de Medici, provided a seminal force in the development of Renaissance thought and culture. These eighteen tracts of the Corpus Hermeticum, along with the Perfect Sermon (also called the Asclepius), are the foundational documents of the Hermetic tradition.

The Emerald Tablet (also known as *Tabula Smaragdina* or *The Secret of Hermes*) is a text that reveals the secret of the primordial substance and its transmutations. The original source of the *Emerald Tablet* is unknown. Although Hermes Trismegistus is the author named in the text, its first known appearance is in a book written in Arabic between the sixth and eighth centuries. In esoteric circles, *The Emerald Tablet* is said to explain the secrets of the creation of beings and the knowledge of the causes of all things. In the mythology surrounding the origin of the book, it is told that Apollonius of Tyana, a first-century philosopher, declared how he discovered Hermes' tomb and claims to have found inside a tomb, an old man sitting on a throne holding the emerald tablet. The Adepts believe that this tablet is the work of Hermes Trismegistus (a combination of the Greek god "Hermes" and the Egyptian god "Toth").

At this point, it is important to emphasize an important aspect of Gnosticism. Creativity and imagination play crucial roles in the transmission of Gnosis. You can make contact with the spirit worlds through the correct use of your imagination. In fact, as the author has hinted earlier in this book, dry intellectual words and information do not contain the precious waters of life that are necessary to transmit wisdom. Your mind responds to that which engages it through your senses and emotions. For example, a myth faithfully told (and not watered down for children or to be socially acceptable) carries more powerful spiritual energy than a scholarly discourse about the myth. The scholarly discourse can amplify and assist you in your appreciation of the myth, but only after you hear the myth and it begins to work inside you. Always it is best if you actually "hear" the myth spoken out of the mouth of an expert storyteller.

Other important Gnostic scriptures that were not found at Nag Hammadi also survived the attempts of the Roman Catholic church to destroy all remnant of Gnostic teachings. Some of these Gnostic scriptures are:

The Hymn of Judas Thomas the Apostle in India

The Acts of Peter and Paul

The Book of Revelation: The Two Witnesses

Pistis Sophia

Hymn of the Pearl

Odes of Solomon

First Book of Ieou and others.

Tragically, Christianity today only accepts the four traditional gospels found in the New Testament. These four Gospels - Matthew, Mark, Luke and John - were extensively edited and censored. There exists no original copy of any of the four Gospels in the New Testament. The four traditional Gospels the world has today are the result of years of copying and compiling by scribes who added and deleted as they saw fit. These four traditional Gospels are also full of errors, as making mistakes is normal when human beings copy a manuscript numerous times and embellish the text for their personal reasons. In addition, Christ Jesus spoke a language called Aramaic. While He was born Jewish and could read the Hebrew sacred texts, it is probable that He did not speak Hebrew with his Apostles or with those people who came to hear Him speak. For, it was not common during the time of Christ Jesus for the Jewish people to speak in Hebrew. Extremely few people in ancient times could read or write. The Jewish people of the time of Christ Jesus spoke Aramaic. The New Testament Gospels, on the other hand, were written in Greek. Thus, before even beginning to speak about all the errors created by innumerable scribes re-copying the Gospels over and over again, one must confront the fact that when Christ Jesus spoke, he spoke in Aramaic. Biblical scholars know that the authors of the Gospels in the New Testament were not the persons traditionally named as the authors of these Gospels: Saint Mark did not write the Gospel of Mark; Saint Matthew did not write the Gospel of Matthew and so on. In order to create each one of the New Testament Gospels, some author who spoke and wrote in Greek had to have read a document already written in Aramaic (or possibly Hebrew, although this is unlikely), or possibly sat and listened as one of the Apostles or followers of Christ Jesus related the stories to him in Aramaic and then the author who spoke and wrote in Greek, translated the Aramaic tales into Greek. So, straightaway, you realize that it is impossible that you are reading the exact words of Christ Jesus; the best that you can hope for is that you are reading the best translation of Christ Jesus' words from Aramaic, into Greek and finally into English.

Plagiarism was not considered blameworthy in the ancient world. Authors freely copied from predecessors without recognition. Thus, the world has no idea about what outside materials, and other teachings, were added to the four authorized Gospels of the New Testament. On the other hand, the age and authenticity of the Nag Hammadi texts are not disputed. They were not subjected to two-thousand years of translating, editing, embellishing and re-copying as were the four traditional Gospels. These Nag Hammadi Gospels, and other writings found at Nag Hammadi, challenge the long-held precepts of the Roman Catholic Church, as well as the Christian churches (Lutheran, Baptist, Anglican, Methodist, Presbyterian, Evangelical and the like) of today. The Roman Catholic Church and Christian churches are unwilling, unprepared and reluctant to accept these long-hidden gospels. The Nag Hammadi manuscripts are still being researched, discussed and translated by different experts. The Gnostic Gospels do not focus so much on the actions of Jesus, but rather on his teachings, namely, on his wisdom. However, delightfully, they talk about a Jesus who laughs, plays as a young child and dances. These stories give the public many more details about the life of Jesus than are found in the four authorized Gospels.

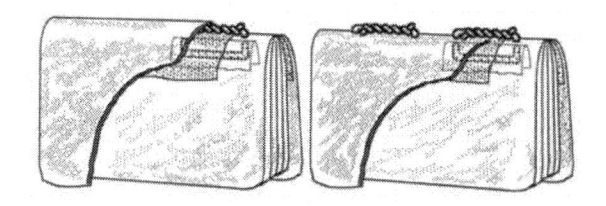

WHAT GOSPEL IS THE TRUE GOSPEL?

Christianity did not begin as a monolithic revelation. In other words, it did not begin as a single teaching directly coming from the mouth of Jesus. After Jesus' death, there were many different and opposing viewpoints concerning who he was and what he taught. There were many different groups competing for converts. Each of these diverse groups traced their teaching back to the individual apostles and each had books to support their points of view. As the Roman Catholic Church gained power, they showed little regard for diversity and eventually destroyed numerous Gnostic texts and nearly killed all the followers of Gnosticism.

The first *Gospel of Mark* was written forty years after the death of the Master Jesus. However, the original document, the first actual handwritten *Gospel of Mark* does not exist anywhere in the world. What humanity does have are copies of copies of Mark's Gospel. By 200 CE, there were up to fifty different gospels in existence. During the first three hundred years after Jesus' death, there was neither an organized religion nor a central authority or book. There were many different opinions and beliefs about who Jesus was. At first, even the apostles argued among themselves and had strong disagreements with the "apostle" Paul (a man who had never met Jesus) over the basic concepts of Jesus' teachings. The Christian Bible as the public knows it, more or less today, did not appear until the middle of the 3rd century. Put differently, the first version of the Christian Bible as the public know it did not appear until about one hundred and twenty years after Jesus died. And St. John's *Book of Revelation* was not accepted as part of the New Testament until 382 CE!

HOW DID THIS HAPPEN?

Emperor Constantine the Great created a formal Christian religion. It is amazing and frightening to ponder the fact that a political leader was the person to formalize Christianity. His first task was the Council of Arles in 314 CE. Constantine the Great attended the Council of Arles along with thirty-three bishops and, during this Council, approved various canons or judgments.

Constantine wanted to establish a world or universal religion, with himself at the head. During this council, he declared his divinity by stating that the God of Christians was his personal sponsor. He then replaced certain Christian religious practices of the time with familiar Roman Empire practices of sun worship along with other Pagan teachings from Syria and Persia. In the year 313 CE., Constantine the Great promulgated the *Edict of Milan* (in Latin, *Edictum Mediolanense*), also known as the *Tolerance of Christianity* which legalized the Christian religion. He continued his work of creating his unique "Catholic" church by organizing a committee of bishops and inviting them to a council held in Nicaea in 325 CE.

Emperor Constantine physically placed himself in the center of this meeting. After weeks of debate, the emperor along with the bishops began the process of selecting precisely those books that did not threaten the power of the state ... alternatively stated, the gospels acceptable to the government. Constantine decided which Gospels and Epistles he approved. This process of creating the Bible reached a milestone with the writing of the *Codex Vaticanus* in the Vatican Library, probably written in Rome in 340 CE by Alexandrian scribes for the Emperor Caesar Constans (the youngest son of Constantine the Great).

Later, Athanasius the Apostolic (the twentieth bishop of Alexandria and one of the attendees at Nicaea in 325 CE) is the first to identify the same twenty-seven New Testament books in use today. The Bible then is a mixed-bag of works assembled by a committee and not the complete set of gospels and epistles that were in existence at that time. All other gospels (for example, the Gnostic gospels) were immediately considered heresy and anyone who owned one was subject to the death penalty.

What was so threatening about these Gnostic gospels and writings that made them worthy of being banned and repressed by the emperor and bishops? What threatened the beginnings of the Roman Catholic Church? In a word: Gnosticism. The religious and political leaders wanted a new church run by male priests, a new church that suppressed the role of women in the church, a new church that crushed the old religions that held the Goddess in great respect. Why did the church do this? The church attacked Gnosticism because the Gnostics taught that the human being does not need a priest, in other words, an intermediary, between him or her and God. The Gnostics also taught about the Divine Feminine (the feminine aspect of the godhood) and that She was as important as the masculine "Father" God and the masculine "Son" of God. Today, Roman Catholic, Protestant and Evangelical churches continue to repress Gnosticism and pretend that the Gnostic Gospels are not worth reading.

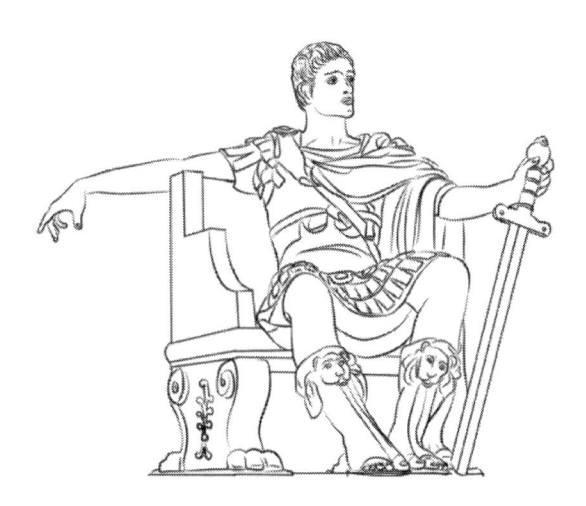

THERE THEY WILL BE CALLED "CHILDREN OF THE LIVING GOD"

The *Royal Library of Alexandria* or *Ancient Library of Alexandria* in Alexandria, Egypt, was one of the largest and most important libraries in the ancient world. The library was created in the third century before the lifetime of Christ Jesus. The Catholic Church considered the pre-Christian contents of the Library of Alexandria to be heretical. Paganism (pre-Christian spiritual belief and practice) was made illegal by "Theodosian decrees" during the years of 389 to 392 CE of Emperor Theodosius I. In 393 CE he issued a comprehensive law that prohibited the public display of all non-Christian religious customs.

The temples of Alexandria were closed by Patriarch Theophilus of Alexandria in 391 CE. The historian Socrates of Constantinople describes that all pagan temples in Alexandria were destroyed, including the famous Serapeum. Experts say there were over a million manuscripts in the library. The Roman Catholic Church burned the library and 95% of the scrolls were lost. The wisdom, history, technology, science, philosophy and knowledge of humanity were destroyed in 391 CE by the Roman Catholic Church. The Muslim conquest of Egypt in 642 CE destroyed almost all of the remaining manuscripts. Nevertheless, you must remember that

Gnosticism is a Mystery religion, in other words, it reveals esoteric knowledge of the deepest mysteries of the universe. This knowledge is given to humankind as a gift from the Supreme Being directly. Gnostics learn about the secrets of the mind and its relationship with the material universe. The Christos taught secret teachings to his closest apostles. In the *Gospel of Judas*, Judas tells the Master:

I know who you are and where you have come from. You are from the immortal realm of Barbelo. And I am not worthy to utter the name of the one who has sent you. [Barbelo is often depicted as a supreme female principle, the single passive antecedent of creation in its manifoldness. Barbelo is also variously referred to as 'Mother-Father' (hinting at her apparent androgyny).]

Judas knew that the Christos was an Aeon and that He came from the Pleroma. Gnostics do not have a Bible, or set of rules or doctrines. Gnosticism is first and foremost a spiritual practice. And while the authorities managed to set fire to the Library of Alexandria, they could not destroy all the pre-Christian writings existing throughout the world. Gnosticism includes the secret teachings that were erased and censored from the book that has become known as The New Testament Bible, and these secret teachings were buried in the sands of Egypt and are known today as the Nag Hammadi Library. The Gnostic teachings are for everyone, regardless of the person's religious or spiritual background and regardless of a person's culture or race. Gnostics reveal:

That which is Below corresponds to that which is Above, and that which is Above corresponds to that which is Below, to accomplish the miracle of the One Thing.

They teach the Divinity of Humanity. Gnostic manuscripts lead people to an understanding of themselves as sons and daughters of God, sharing God's Divinity. In the *Gospel of Thomas*, the Christos says:

"When you come to know yourselves, then you will become known and you will realize that it is you who are the sons of the living father. But if you will not know yourselves, you dwell in poverty and it is you who are that poverty."

RESURRECTION

Those who say that the Lord died first and then rose up are in error, for he rose up first and then died. If one does not first attain the resurrection, he will not die.

Gospel of Philip

The Gnostics believed that everyone can experience resurrection before death. In other words, Gnostics are granted such special knowledge that they can regenerate their bodies and resurrect themselves before dying. Moreover, they have special abilities to control their DNA.

Matthew 17: 1-2 reads as follows:

After six days, Jesus took with him Peter, James and John his brother and brought them up into a high mountain by themselves. He was changed before them. His face shone like the sun, and his garments became as white as the light.

The Sufi Dervishes know and teach these practices. Additionally, in *Dzogchen* (a teaching from the *Nyingma* school of Tibetan Buddhism) they speak of the "Rainbow Body". The exceptional practitioners of Dzogchen, when they are about to die, concentrate on their Body of Pure Light. His or her physical body releases itself into a body of non-material light (a *Sambhogakaya*) with the capacity to exist and to remain where and when indicated by one's compassion. In Gnosticism, this is called the radiant body, resurrection body, or immortal body (the *soma athanaton*). This body has also been called "The Philosopher's Stone".

YOU ARE THE PLEROMA

Humankind creates the world. In the ultimate analysis, it is humanity that creates angels, archangels, demons, gods, goddesses and devils. The *Gospel of Philip* divulges:

God created the human being. [. . .] human beings create God. That is the way it is in the world – humans make gods and worship their creation. It would be fitting for the gods to worship human beings!

Can you overcome the programming that has obstructed you from seeing this truth? School, television, radio, Internet, bad parenting, social media, newspapers, magazines, all contribute to the blinding of your sight and are dominated by the Alien Parasites.

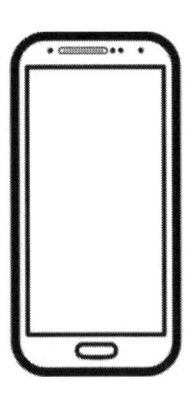

WHAT IS REAL?

There's nothing solid in the world. Everything that looks solid is nothing more than vibration moving at a very fast pace. Scientists have discovered that reality consists of 99.999% empty space. When they examined the atoms that make up any physical object, they discovered that only 0.001% of atoms are physical particles and that the other 99.999% of atoms consist of empty space. That empty space is filled with a mysterious energy. This "mysterious energy" is consciousness. Conscience creates everything. Each person experiences an illusion of physicality. The mind weaves together selected information contained in the energy field in a manner designed to keep the individual alive in order to reproduce. This is similar to how an individual weaves a carpet utilizing various colorful threads. And this process of weaving this carpet of conscious energy or information produces and creates what people call reality. Is it possible that the Creator could hurt or damage His/Her creation? The Supreme Reality (who can also be recognized as the Master Programmer) is pure and infinite love. However, when you focus on the Aeons or any of the lower creators (programmers) below, the answer is "yes". Why? For example, think of the author of a novel or graphic novel. It is not unusual for novels to contain deaths, wars, accidents, illnesses, suicides and the like. People like duality. The public really appreciates a good villain and a courageous hero who confronts him or her. In the duality of the novel, you feel enjoyment. The novel is a world unto itself, as is a computer game. The beings and characters in a novel often suffer quite severely. Even in some science fiction novels, the entire Planet Earth is destroyed. The author creates his or her own apocalypse.

The people, murders, wars and so on in these books are not real. They're just words on a page. These words are information you receive when you read the book. You mind weaves these words and creates images and gives you the sense that you are living in the world of books. However, this "book world" is only a fictitious reality. No one's actually hurt. Evil will disappear when you stop being so fascinated by it. What fascinates you to the news media (newspapers, cable, internet, and so forth)? The answer is: murder, rape, assassinations, bombings, thefts, shootings, war, train wrecks, and the list goes on and on. When you stop looking at evil, when you stop believing in evil, evil will stop being "fed" and will shrivel away. There can be no "ultimate evil" because the Ultimate of Everything is the One Absolute Being. Humans have no more than an inkling of the meaning or purpose, of life. What appears evil, may in reality, be good. Hypothetically, imagine encountering a situation in which you see a woman cutting off the leg of a man. The man is screaming in agony. Obviously, what she is doing is wrong and terrible. What do you do? You probably would attempt to stop the woman, or if that did not seem feasible, you would call the police. Then when the police arrive an officer takes you aside and explains to you that the woman is a surgeon and she is removing the gangrenous leg of the man. You might feel foolish under those circumstances, for when the officer provided you with more information, the entire context of what was occurring between the woman and the man changed. How many times do you make this mistake every week of your life, assuming that someone is doing something horrible, when in fact they are behaving for the highest good? The man in the speeding car, who is driving erratically, cuts you off in traffic and you begin to scream curses at him; but then you discover that he is rushing his son who is unconscious in the back seat to the Emergency Room because the boy cannot breathe due to a severe asthma attack. If you truly believe that the Absolute is Unknowable, as so many of the Nag Hammadi texts describe, then you are forced to admit that you do not know the full context and ramification of every "bad" event that happens in the world. Just as no atheist can state unequivocally that God does not exist, because that would presuppose that the atheist is All-Knowing; so too, no spiritual person can state unequivocally that someone is evil, for that would presuppose that the spiritual person is All-Knowing. Focus on making yourself a better person, and that will do more good for the world than indulging yourself in ghastly and horrid news stories.

For those of you who might think that this concept that you are living in a computer simulation is absurd, just pause for a moment and watch some videos on the Internet about the latest advances in robotics. Today, there exist robots in the form of human beings, some of which can imitate facial expressions of men and women to an astonishing degree. Still others are being trained as warriors, to fight on the battlefields of the future. Some countries are already using drones, with artificial intelligence, to make firing decisions (kill decisions) without human involvement.

Genetically modified livestock and other animals have existed for over twenty years. In 2015 the *Food and Drug Administration* approved the sale of genetically modified salmon. As this book is being written, gene editing companies and biotechnology lobbyists are trying to convince the current administration to move the regulation of GE (genetically edited) livestock to the *U.S. Department of Agriculture* (USDA). If that happens, genetically modified meat might soon show up in grocery stores near you. Most of the meat sold in restaurants and supermarkets comes from animals raised on genetically modified foods. Most dairy products sold in supermarkets (unless specified) contain rBGH (Recombinant Bovine Growth Hormone), including milk, cheese, butter, yogurt, ice cream and buttermilk. Many countries have animals in the laboratory that are a genetic mixture of several animals. These animals are called *chimeras*. Chimpanzees do not have a legal status and if they pose a threat to humans they are killed. If a chimpanzee is genetically altered to be more like a human, it can blur the ethical line between animal and man. There is a great deal of evidence showing that chimpanzee-human chimeras have already been created. It is not illogical to imagine that in the next ten years or so, scientists will begin to create intelligent apes to do the manual labor that humans do today. Eventually, people will be able to create (or buy) their own genetically modified biological robots so that they can act out game scenarios (like what the video games of today can do now). This would be similar to a nightmarish version of "human chess" often seen at Renaissance fairs.

Maybe all this will start as a harmless chess game played with monkeys implanted with a Brain Computer Interface (BCI). But where will it end? The "Project Pandora" of the *Central Intelligence Agency* (CIA), one of the largest intelligence agencies of the United States Government, uses *Radio Remote Brain Manipulation* demonstrating that the human brain can be remotely controlled by the use of microwave beams.

You have the ability, through spiritual practices (yoga, meditation, prayer, fasting, singing and so on and so forth), to see beyond this world in which you live every day. It is possible to find beauty. Walt Whitman wrote in Leaves of Grass:

I swear to you there are divine things more beautiful than words can tell.

Beauty transports you to levels of awareness that go beyond your daily life. Do not let your compassion for those suffering in the world to blind your eyes to the beauty that also exists.

There is so much beauty in the world, but you must allow yourself to see it.

Tom Giaquinto

So, your will is the key. You have the choice as to what world you want to experience. If you do not seek for beauty, you will only encounter ugliness. However, if you do encounter beauty, you will encounter a World that has been called a "Name of God."

Beauty is truth, truth beauty

John Keats

Beauty is the key to Cosmic Consciousness. Beauty is a sender. In other words, beauty carries you directly to the Pleroma. There's no beauty in the false, the artificial and the lie.

Most of the "physical" world cannot be seen. Scientists can only see approximately 5% of the universe using all their scientific instruments and equipment. Reality consists of much more than what you can perceive with your senses. All Reality is Consciousness!

HAVE NO FEAR

You have the power to defeat any Alien Parasites. You have divine authority over all creation because you are intimately joined with the Christos and Sophia. You are more unique than you can possibly imagine. You are so unique that your way to enlightenment is the only way, for you and you only. Everyone else, if they exist, have their own paths.

At first, you must be willing to enter a state of liminality. In other words, you must be willing to enter a state in which you stand on the threshold and are no longer grasping the worldviews and sense of yourself that you held in the past, nor yet completely ready to enter the Kingdom of Heaven. You stand on the threshold, the doorsill, neither in one world nor another. This can be a frightening place to be. However, if you are practicing the methods in this book carefully and correctly, there is no fear.

Ultimately, for those who desire states of Gnosis (direct spiritual knowledge) and illumination, you must transcend all simulations. Through gradually letting go of each simulation in which you find yourself, you can eventually attain states of enlightenment. You gradually peel away the layers. In a way, it is like when someone asks you to play a game with them, and you say "No." The other person may attempt to persuade you in various ways to play the game, but if you are firm and unshakeable and refuse to play, eventually they will go away. All spiritual seekers have read the words of various great gurus and Initiates that teach that the person on the path of knowledge must let go of all attachment to the world. This author would like to update this and say that the seeker must let go of all of his or her attachments to simulations if his or her ultimate goal is to reach the Ultimate Reality.

A fascinating experience awaits those who are willing to make this ultimate renunciation: these dedicated people discover that they receive in return all that they have ever wanted and more. This experience too is spoken about by the great sages of all time. Be careful to include in your renunciations all your most embarrassing secrets, traumas, most shameful deeds and all the ways you harm yourself. In other words, do not hold onto past embarrassments in a misguided attempt to "atone for your sins." As Pema Chödrön, an American nun in the Kagyu lineage of Tibetan Buddhism, teaches, that people must let go of "*holding back.*" She says that the spiritual seeker must renounce "*closing down and shutting off from life.*"

In your meditations, call to mind yourself. As you choose to be aware of your "you," explore this self of yours. Ask yourself, "Who am I?" Many folks respond by thinking about what they do, for example, "I am a scientist." Or they think about their personality, for example, "I am a kind person." The greatest Sufi poet Rumi said,

I looked for God. I went to a temple and did not find him there. I went to a church and did not find him there. I went to a mosque and did not find him there. Finally, I looked in my heart, and there he was.

Conceptual labels that you associate with yourself are not your Self. For, is not "God" as you used to know "Him" (through traditional religion), in its microcosmic aspect, a projection of your thoughts and imaginations of your very self? Tony Crisp at dreamhawk.com writes,

Therefore, the god archetype is an expression of what we sense as our own potential and of the enormity of life and cosmic processes out of which we have existence.

Some contemporary Gnostics hold to the mythos that the Absolute Reality had some sort of "emotional/mental breakdown" and because of this breakdown, evil entered the Universe in the form of Sophia's "fall" from the Pleroma, as well as the creation of the Demiurge and the Archons. Yet, if you believe that the Absolute Reality is Infinite, it must have integrity (the state of being whole and undivided).

You can call this integrity by the name: consistency. Regardless of how you choose to look at it, the Christos was very clear when He taught:

Every kingdom divided against itself, is brought to naught, and every city or house divided against itself shall not stand.

Matthew 12:25

Consequently, the Absolute Reality cannot be divided against itself. Duality cannot exist ultimately. By its very definition, the One Reality must be whole and undivided. This is why you need not fear, for you contain a spark of Divinity and that Divinity is One, and nothing can exist apart from that One. If a person or an Archon attacks you, they are attacking the entire Universe. Your task is to cultivate a realization of the integrity of the universe.

Peace comes from the absence of fear, from a consciousness of trust, from a deep, underlying faith in the absolute goodness and mercy, the final integrity of the universe in which we live and of every cause to which we give our thought, our time and our attention.

Ernest Holmes

DREAMS ARE THE WORLDS YOU CREATE

The late spiritual teacher, Bubba Free John (born Franklin Albert Jones, and also known as Adi Da Love-Ananda Samraj, wrote:

The waking world is not a 'place,' and 'earth,' but a realm, an indefinite dimension, just as the condition or region into which you enter in dreams is a dimensionless realm.

There is THAT within each human being that creates dreams. There is the playwright, the cinematographer. A part of the dreaming person selects which "camera shots" the dreamer will see. Take the time to notice, the next time you remember your dream, from whose perspective you are viewing the activity in the dream. Is it all happening as if you were seeing the action through your eyes, or from the eyes of some person near you, or perhaps all is being seen from a vantage point that places you behind the action? This will give you a clue as to how you see yourself in your daily life, are you the center of your life, the supporting actor, or just one of the "extras"?

While you are dreaming, a part of your spirit also creates other people (sometimes people who are unknown to you), as well as the location, climate, buildings, that exist in the dream. A dream is a world within a world. This indicates that, while you sleep in the "real" world, you are having experiences in another world . . . for example, a world in which you can fly or a world in which you are married to the man or woman of your dreams.

Take a moment to realize that, because you dream, you are a creator. "Story" is a part of the reality of humanity. Dreams have a presence, a force and an emotional impact that commands your attention. Is a dream only a wish that creates a pressure or force that beats against the subconscious, forcing it to construct a dream? For example, you may have an important meeting with your boss at 9:00 am, on Monday morning and you have a dream, concerning the meeting, at approximately 3:00 am, that morning. Almost everyone has had dreams such as these, whether it be the morning of an important school examination, a doctor's visit, a driving test, or some important event. Yet, why does the dream appear to be similar to a movie, theatrical production, or if it is a very vivid dream, indistinguishable from reality? Notice that an intermediate step is missing between the event (the meeting with your boss) and the particular characteristics of the dream. In other words, you might dream that the meeting goes well. You may dream that you show up to the meeting in your underwear! Or your dream may have you spending more with the boss's secretary than with the boss or the subject of the meeting. Something or someone takes the known facts, that is to say that at 9:00 am, you and your boss are going to meet in his office for a meeting and then creates an entire narrative involving the upcoming event.

As Jungian analyst Marie-Louise von Franz says in *The Way of the Dream,*

> *Dreams are the letters of the Self that the Self writes us every night.*

Who is awake within yourself while you are asleep? There is a witness who does not rest who is inseparable from your life. This witness watches everything that occurs in your waking state as though it were a dream. THAT witness is aware. Scientists tell the public that during dream sleep their highest cognitive functions shut down, allowing other aspects of the human brain (that evolved in much more ancient times) to express themselves. In other words, during sleep, the ego steps aside permitting humans to tap into the more ancient wisdom that predates egoic perspectives.

From an analysis of any person's dreams it is obvious that dreams display a story and a sub-text. Dreams have their own sort of logic and congruency, which flies in the face of some biologists' position that dreams are nothing more than neural reflux. These biologists propose that dreams are just the nightly garbage dump of daily neuron activity. The powers of imagination residing in the mind are nothing less than astounding. The subconscious decides to give you a dream. Why do you see that particular dream movie? The subconscious acts as a brilliant playwright coming up with fantastic and deeply significant scenarios. Resident within each human being is a deeply ingrained natural drive toward resolution, solution and the fulfillment of desires. Humanity wants to know the meaning of life and maintains a continuous dialogue every night with various aspects of their being in order to receive answers to their most pressing questions. For those individuals who are interacting with lofty spiritual beings through daily meditation and ritual, these individuals receive information directly from the Indivisible Consciousness which gives the individual's spirit the power and force to complete his or her mission during the period of "dreamless" sleep.

Jung maintained that a crucial factor in determining how conscious you are is whether you attends to your dreams, and the degree to which this enables you to make what is unconscious conscious. By working with dreams, you "create soul," you "wake up" to your total situation, become conscious and achieve wholeness.

Many people practice "lucid dreaming". This is a practice that almost everyone can learn. During a lucid dream, you "wake up" in your dream. Simply put, you are aware that you are dreaming, and consequently can influence the course and outcome of your dream. People think the mundane world is dense and three-dimensional, yet when it is seen with the eyes of Truth, it is no more genuine, essential, established, or important, than the dream world. Is dreaming not also a way of consciously creating a universe?

THE ROLE OF WOMEN IN GNOSTICISM

Sophia's story is the most repressed story in the history of the world. Men have traditionally controlled Christianity. First, they affirmed that only men can become priests, bishops, cardinals and popes. Even some passages of the New Testament that Roman Catholics, Christians and Evangelicals read today in their churches are blatantly anti-female. For instance, the counsel of St. Paul in *1 Timothy 2:12* in which the saint says:

> *But I don't permit a woman to teach, nor to exercise authority over a man, but to be in quietness.*

and Ephesians 5:22:

> *Wives, be subject to your own husbands, as to the Lord.*

are two examples of how men seized power in the early Christian church.

This demotion of the exalted role of the Divine Feminine and the role of women in spirituality is nothing less than a horrible nightmare that Western Society has been experiencing for a very long time. It is the wound that will not heal, as spoken of in the Arthurian Romances. It may be helpful to examine some of the basic facts in order to understand how humanity has been so severely injured.

From the beginning of the human race, circa 200,000 BC, there arose only matriarchal societies. They reflect the initial and most natural behavior of women, men, old and young.

The first humans gradually spread over the whole planet. And on their voyages, they left behind wonderful art and symbolic language - in caves, on objects - that tell humanity their story. Some of them continued with their lifestyle until today - using the same patterns and symbols on their pottery, clothes and so on. The Neolithic people refined their cultures from 10,000 BC in North and South America, in Near East, East Asia and Middle East. In these places the later Advanced Cultures independently evolved. Matriarchies lasted until approximately 2500 BC when conquerors moved West, East and South East from Inner Asia.

Horse riding conquering hordes, the Indo-Europeans, had to leave their fertile land that became dry prairies. The climate changed during centuries and when the Indo-Europeans wandered and came to good soil, they had to reestablish their daily life and social structures. After some decades of increasing dryness and lack of rain they had to move again and again. This happened for generations and in cases of privation, humans tend to return to a previous state of civilization. The females and children lived together and the males built their own groups, who moved forward to find water and food.

At last, those already patriarchal organized men-groups (maybe some with women) bumped into to wealthy matriarchal cultures. Their own skills of civilization were long lost in the fight of pure survival. Matriarchal societies consisted of peaceful people. That means: the archaeological evidence has found that matriarchal societies show no signs of violence, crime, war, nor weapons.

Some matriarchal cities or tribes could probably integrate the foreigners, others became simply subdued. But nobody could withstand the dominating, unscrupulous people who arrived like waves crashing against matriarchy. Eventually, in many cultures, a beautiful form of equality took shape. Men and women lived in harmony, with no one sex assuming control. However, as you know, eventually men, perhaps through sheer force, took control, and by the time of Christ Jesus were well on their way to full dominance of society and religion. There are still many living peoples with matriarchal structures on all continents, and evidence has been presented to the author that ancient Gnostic groups still continue to this day in Italy and Sicily.

Women have a beautiful and central role to play in Gnostic spirituality. Gnostics have a great devotion to Sophia (Gaia), Barbelo, as well as to Mary the Mother of Jesus and Mary Magdalene. No people dwelling on any continent began as a patriarchal culture from their very beginning.

WHAT HAPPENED TO "THE DIVINE FEMININE"?

What happened to the Divine Feminine? Why has She apparently disappeared from Judaism, Christianity and Islam? The Gnostic Gospels, teach that Mary Magdalene was probably the closest disciple of the Christos, the one whom the Master taught the most arcane esoteric wisdom. She was and is the representation of all wisdom. The male apostles of the Christos demonstrated both their jealousy and respect for the wisdom and position of Mary Magdalene. For example, in *The Gospel According to Mary Magdalene*, the following passage may be found in which the disciple ask Mary:

Tell us the words of the Savior which you remember which you know, but we do not, nor have we heard them. Mary answered and said, "What is hidden from you I will proclaim to you."

Mary Magdalene through her connection with Wisdom shows her identification with Sophia. Christos and Sophia were a divine couple, divine consorts, who came directly from the Pleroma. A consort is a kind of counterpart. The Catholic Church and later the Protestant, Christian and Evangelical churches have sought to destroy all traces of Her majesty, Her divine wisdom and Her role as consort of the Christos. The more you develop devotion to

Sophia, the more you will be protected from all kinds of polluting thoughts that Alien Parasites attempt to insert into your mind.

Remember that, according to the *Gospel of John*, there were "Three Marys" at the foot of the Cross!

Mary, Mother of Jesus

Mary of Clopas

Mary Magdalene

Three women mentioned in *Mark 16: 1* also came to the tomb of Jesus who were named "Mary"!

Mary Magdalene

Mary of Clopas

Maria Salome the Disciple

In Spanish-speaking countries, the asterism of Orion's belt is called "Las Tres Marías" (The Three Marys).

Christianity borrowed heavily from pre-Christian indigenous spiritual beliefs, one of the most important indigenous beliefs is that of the Triple Goddess. The three female goddesses are often described as the Maiden, the Mother and the Crone, each of which symbolizes a separate stage in the female life cycle and a phase of the Moon.

The Sophianic narrative cannot be received as information that you read in books and on the Internet. You must fill yourself with the spiritual vitality of Gnosticism. This true Gnosticism is not defiled by the patriarchal, hateful and misogynistic contaminations of the Catholic and Christian Churches. Patriarchal religion is an extraterrestrial virus: the masterpiece of the Demiurge.

Mother Mary represents Sophia in her role as Mother Goddess or Gaia. Carl Jung shared this insight:

Blue is the color of Mary's celestial cloak; she is the earth covered by the blue tent of the sky

It is impossible, even in patriarchal religions such as Judaism, Christianity and Islam (which have dominated the Earth for the last three thousand years) to repress the Divine Feminine, also called *The Goddess* or *Feminine Aspect of God*. One way or another, the sacred feminine will manifest itself, even in patriarchal religions. Mary Magdalene represents Sophia in her role as the consort of Jesus. The *Gospel According to Mary Magdalene* was in all probability not written by Mary Magdalene, but Mary Magdalene is the prominent figure found everywhere in the Gospel. She was an advanced Initiate into the Christos' secret teachings unknown to the male disciples. The *Gospel of Philip* dates from the 2nd or 3rd century AD. This gospel contains the following quote:

And the companion of the [...] Mary Magdalene. [...] loved her more than all the disciples, and used to kiss her often on her mouth. The rest of the disciples [...]. They said to him "Why do you love her more than all of us?" The Savior answered and said to them, "Why do I not love you like her? When a blind man and one who sees are both together in darkness, they are no different from one another. When the light comes, then he who sees will see the light and he who is blind will remain in darkness."

The great error of the Catholic Church, the Protestant, Christian and Evangelical churches is that they preach a Christos devoid of his consort: Sophia. These churches are teaching an unbalanced representation of the Divine Emanation. This "imbalance" is evidence of the activity of the Archons working inside the churches.

Throughout history there have been many "Marian apparitions": such as the Shrine of Guadalupe in Mexico, the Shrine of Fatima in Portugal and the Shrine of Lourdes in France. According to Christian tradition, on October 12, A.D. 40, the Mary appeared to the apostle James the Great in the municipality of Zaragoza. This apparition is called "La Virgen del Pilar". Mary is invoked under this title as the patron saint of Spain, of the *Spanish Civil Guard* and of the Hispanic world. Approximately in 1392, She appeared to two indigenous shepherds in Tenerife (Canary Islands, Spain). This apparition is known as the *Virgin of Candelaria*. On Sunday, July 2, 1962, four girls in Garabandal met the apparition of the Blessed Mother accompanied by two angels, one of them St. Michael and the other unknown. It is impossible to repress the Divine Feminine.

HOW TO PROTECT YOURSELF FROM THE ARCHONS

You now know that there exists evil beings called Archons (Alien Parasites), which are not alive like you are; they are more like cybernetic organisms than human beings. So, how do you protect yourself from the Archons? One important method is to avoid labyrinthine conspiracy theories and thoughts you cannot stop. A complex and complicated book is good because it exercises the mind. However, if this book leads you to obsess over it, thinking about it day and night, it is harmful. Evil loves complications, labyrinths and byzantine conspiracy theories. Ernest Holmes wrote:

The truth is simple, direct and always self-evident.

If your mind feels like you are on a hamster wheel, then stop! You are putting yourself in danger the more you involve yourself in endless mazes. It is fine if you enjoy studying and investigating a particular subject or religion, explore conspiracy theories and take pleasure in reading books, watching movies, playing a musical instrument, participating in sports and exercise, listening to live music and enjoying life. However, you must not become obsessed with any of these. Do not become so engrossed in details that you lose sight of the goal. In life, you need a mission, purpose and intention to energize your work. However, obsession drains your energy. Remember, life is a spectrum; enjoy the polychromatic colors of life's joys and pleasures.

ALIEN PARASITES AND HUMANITY'S CHILDREN

Alien Mind Parasites are attacking children! Alien Parasites attack children through violent video games, music videos with lyrics and images of adult sexuality, drug use, denigration of and violence toward women! Horribly, even children's cartoons are now filled with the above shocking, repulsive and obscene images. Children are being bombarded with electrical and chemical contamination in food, beverages, cell phones and microwave transmitters. The Alien Parasites are turning children into materialistic, violent, Godless puppets.

By the time a teenager graduates from high school, they have seen 8,000 real or simulated murders in movies, the Internet, video games and television. This negative imagery is the perfect insertion vehicle for Alien Parasites to enter the child's brain. If you care about your children - protect them from Alien Parasite attacks. Prevent your child from becoming addicted to media that is full of torture, murder, blood, bullets and violence. Beware of anything that generates negative emotions!

MORE DETAILS ABOUT THE ARCHONS

Paul Chen, in his article *Human Oversight of Self-Awareness Reveals Manipulative Extraterrestrial Presence* the journalist for *THE CANADIAN* newspaper, writes that:

Gnostics detected the Archons as physical intruders into our biosphere, that also used their technological sophistication as artificial intelligences, to manipulate the human psyche, so as to operate, as a parasitic "shadow" on the human consciousness.

The Gnostics referred to the Archons as an "artificial man." Archon, has linguistic origins in Greek, in reference to "authority," and comes from the same root as "arch," as in "archangel."

The Gnostics specifically used the term 'Archons' in reference to the idea of these artificial sentient beings, as "fallen angels" that, inhibit spiritual awakening by convincing humanity of a false reality, forces of sin and temptation. Gnostics represent the Archons as indeed as seeking to inspire systems of organized religion, and other corresponding authority structures.

The Archons are the servants of the Demiurge. The Archons are ruling spirits, but they are false rulers. They are intermediate spirits. Archons are imitators who cannot produce anything original, but arrogantly claim that they can produce something new and creative. Some say the Archons are the beings referred to in Genesis 6:2:

God's sons saw that men's daughters were beautiful, and they took any that they wanted for themselves.

Archons are basically cosmic bureaucrats. They are demons. In short, they are the Alien Parasites. The Archons are in people's minds and brains. They love to help people make mistakes, to the point that people are completely lost in confusion. Archons love to lead people into labyrinths of confusion and excessive complexity. Archons want you to become obsessed with yourself. Archons make people think that they (the Archons) are more powerful than humanity. Have hope! Do not give up. The Archons, in fact, are much less powerful than the Aeons who live in the Pleroma. If you strengthen your connection with Sophia, the Christos and the Aeons, you have nothing to fear.

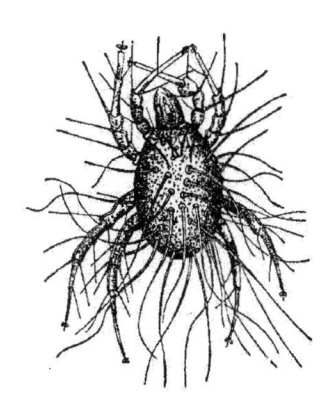

HOW DOES A PERSON ATTRACT ALIEN PARASITES?

This book has explained, in part, how these parasites feed on the energy and negative actions of human beings. In addition, it is essential to know that they enter the mind through excessive abuse of the pleasures of the material world (in other words, through greed, lust, drug addiction, alcoholism, etc.). Note: you should not avoid the pleasures of this world. The Divine wants you to live a life full of pleasure and joy. It is when you cross the line from use to abuse that you attract Alien Parasites.

WHO ARE SOME OF THE MOST FAMOUS GNOSTICS?

Gnosticism, as the author refers to it here, is not primarily a system of beliefs based on the set of writings found at Nag Hammadi or on the teachings of various groups during the early centuries of Christianity. Gnosticism is the collection of wisdom teachings passed down through the ages. Jose M. Herrou Aragon wrote,

Primordial Gnosis is always present, although there are many who are not aware of it. In the different circumstances in which it has appeared openly in the world, it has always been the same Gnosis, although with different historical and cultural connotations. Primordial Gnosis is the original Gnosis, true Gnosis, eternal Gnosis, Gnostic knowledge in its pure form. Due to multiple persecutions, Primordial Gnosis has been fragmented, distorted and hidden.

The individuals and groups listed here are some individuals and organizations who have researched, taught and used the concept of a direct experience with the Divine and who experienced their own true divinity. The inner power of life is within you and this inner power is the Divine, and the Divine has all power. Many people and groups mentioned here were Christians and others were not.

Every time a new flower blooms, you are that flower. You are blooming. You are living in an infinite quantum field, so it does not matter in which direction you can choose to view reality - as a hierarchical chain from lowest to highest or a hierarchy from highest to lowest - it does not matter. Because there is an endless blossoming of this flower in all directions. You cannot simply say that you are "ascending upwards" for example, because there is no up or down, right, or left, or diagonal, in the infinite quantum field! Just as you cannot order soup in a restaurant and ask the waiter to please serve each ingredient separately, so too, humanity also lives in a quantum vibratory soup. That is why there is no dogma in Gnosticism. You just need to intensify your consciousness.

This book provides this list of great Gnostics so that you, the reader, can see the great breadth and magnitude of the Gnostic understanding of the world, and how many great minds have used its principles. If you wish, you can continue your study of Gnosticism by reading about the lives and teachings of these individuals and groups.

It is written that the Egyptian beings: Dyehuty (in Greek Tot) and his consort Ma'at first brought the wisdom of the gods to humankind. After them came the Egyptian goddess Isis and her consort Osiris (whom Isis raised from the dead).

Hermes Trismegistus is the most famous Gnostic. He was the founder of the pre-Christian lineage of Greek Gnosticism. He has been credited as one of the founders of the Mystery Teachings and is the one who discovered Alchemy.

After Hermes Trismegistus, Pythagoras is perhaps the second most famous Gnostic. Pythagoras was initiated by a Mongol shaman.

Very noteworthy is the great initiate Rudolf Joseph Laurence Steiner, outstanding scientist and mystic of the last century, father of Anthroposophy and one of the great spiritual adepts of the twentieth century. Steiner was a Gnostic. The author of this book recommends all of Steiner's works.

However, there were many other Great Gnostic Adepts. There are degrees of proximity to the Absolute and various approaches. The author wants to be clear that while he believes each of these people mentioned personified Gnosticism to one degree or another, he does not feel that it is appropriate to comment on each person's degree of attainment. Some of the Gnostic Adepts include (not in chronological order): Pakal "the Great", Enoch, Zoroaster, Orpheus, Lord Krishna and Sri Radha, Viracocha (Wiracocha or Huiracocha), Marcion of Sinope, Mahavatar Babaji, Sara the Black, Grand Sheikh Muzaffer Ozak al-Jerrahi, Master Morya, Lao-Tsu, Quetzalcoatl (feathered serpent), Giovanni Pico Della Mirandola, Philip Kindred Dick, Lord Maitreya, Akhenaten,

Baal Shem Tov, The Count of Saint Germain, Apollonius de Tyana, Sidarta Gautama (better known as Gautama Buddha), Baron Giulio Cesare Andrea Evola, Piotr Demianovich Ouspensky, Moses, Kassia, Master Serapis, Hinmatóowyalahtqi̓t (Thunder rumbling in the mountains) or Great Chief Joseph, Margarita Porete, Mani, William Shakespeare, Stanley Kubrick, Hypatia of Alexandria, Jalal ad-Din Muhammad Rumi, J. R. R. Tolkien, Hadewijch of Antwerp, Johann Wolfgang von Goethe, Mahadeviyamma, Guillaume Belibaste, Ibn al-'Arabi, Juliana of Norwich, Carl Gustav Jung, Mahavir, Master Eckhart, Simon the Magician (also called Simon of Gitta or Simon Magnus), Bahá'u'lláh, Alice A. Bailey, Mitra, Apollonius of Tyana, Annie Besant, Master Djwhal Khul, Tasunka Witko (literally "Crazy Horse" in the Sioux language) the chief and shaman of the Sioux Oglala, Joan of Arc, Osho, John the Baptist, Johannes Valentinus Andreae, Akhenaton, Neferu Atón Nefertiti, Sai Baba (of Shirdi), Valentin the Gnostic, San Nikodemus el Ayiorita, Menandro, Teresa de Ávila, Nicolas and Perenelle Flamel, Ilyas (Elias), Tecla de Iconio, George Ivanovich Gurdjieff, Kabir, Ali Ibn Abi Talib, Master Koot Humi, Fatima az-Zahra (the luminous one), Iamblichus, Marpa, Padmasambhava (Guru Rinpoche) and Yeshe Tsogyal, Milarepa, Rabi'a al-Adawiyya, Patanjali, Ramana Maharshi, Nicholas Roerich and Helena Roerich, Mary or Maria the Jewess (Latin: Maria Prophetissima), Cleopatra the alchemist, Nisargadatta Maharaj, Al-Khidr (the Green), Medera, Taphnutia,

Robert Anton Wilson, Idries Shah, Paracelsus, Isaac Newton, Sir Galahad, Edgar Cayce, Macarius of Corinth, Matsyendra Nath, Alan Watts, Galileo Galilei, Wilhelm Reich, Giordano Bruno, Ernest Holmes, Paracelsus, Madame Helena Petrovna Blavatsky, Lalleshwari, Aleister Crowley, the Prophet Mahomed (also called Muhammad, Mohammed or Mahomet), Neville Goddard, Saint Sarah and Mansur al-Hallaj.

It is mandatory to include also include musicians and composers: Johann Sebastian Bach, Ludwig van Beethoven, Wolfgang Amadeus Mozart, Wilhelm Richard Wagner, Josef Anton Bruckner, Jean Sibelius, Piotr Ilyich Tchaikovsky, Béla Viktor János Bartók, Leoš Janáček, Igor Fyodorovich Stravinsky, Aram Ilyich Khachaturian, Ralph Vaughan Williams and Philip Morris Glass. In addition, the world must not forget the great painters, such as: Rembrandt Harmenszoon van Rijn, Sandro Botticelli, Leonardo di ser Piero da Vinci, William Blake, Salvador Dalí, Michelangelo Buonarroti (in Italian "Michelangelo"), Gustave Moreau, and Vincent Willem van Gogh. The list must also include the great dancers and choreographers in such a list of the Great Gnostic Adepts: Marius Petipa, Mikhail Fokin, Vaslav Nijinsky, Galina Ulanova, Alvin Ailey, Martha Graham, George Balanchine, Margot Fonteyn, Natalia Makarova, and Maurice Béjart. Gabrielle Roth writes:

God is the dance and the dance is the way to freedom and freedom is our holy work.

The author wishes to state that Gnosis is not only confined to the paths the above individuals have taken, but Gnosis can be found through sculpture, photography, gardening, doing time in prison, acting, seclusion, monastic life, and very clearly through the most radical, rebellious of conspiracy theories, people exploring the avant-garde fringe, and those whose work forces them to exist on the margins of society.

Several *mikogami* (precisely women shamans) ruled southwestern Japan in ancient times. Ancient stories inform that the ancient shaman Himiko (or Pimiko) was chosen to rule the kingdom of *Wa* during a period of military anarchy and succeeded in restoring peace. Women shamans were important spiritual and social influences in many East Asian cultures, including ancient China. In the 1600s, the Peruvian Inquisition targeted wise *Quechua* and *Aymara* women, who kept the indigenous religion alive and often acted to empower their communities and protect them from colonial heads and officials.

In 1591, the Brazilian Inquisition prosecuted the Portuguese witch Maria Gonçalves (also known as Burn-tail) for sexual witchcraft and for making powders from forest herbs. She challenged the bishop, saying that, if he preached from the pulpit, she preached from the *cadeira* (priestess chair). Maria Sabina Magdalena Garcia (July 22, 1894, Huautla de Jimenez, Oaxaca - November 23, 1985) was a *curandera* and shaman of the *Mazatec* indigenous ethnicity of the state of Oaxaca in Mexico. She subverted patriarchal theology by invoking the Divine Feminine in her entrancing chants.

BEWARE OF TEACHERS OF GNOSTICISM WHO MAKE OUTRAGEOUS CLAIMS ABOUT THEMSELVES

Some Gnostic experts hold strange, incorrect and extreme opinions that they present in their books and presentations as the one and only explanation of Gnosticism. Beware of people who make scandalous claims for themselves, for example, who claim that they are an avatar, bodhisattva, archangel, or the founder of Gnosticism. Focus on the spiritual books and methods that lead you to know the Divine directly. Do not become obsessed with particular individuals. Rather, focus on what they taught or are teaching. So too, beware of anyone who preaches hatred of any group of people, or who makes you feel uncomfortable.

GNOSTIC CONFESSION?

What is confession? It is a sacrament in the Roman Catholic Church and in some other Christian churches. Ultimately, however, it is a spiritual practice to help understand and be aware of one's thoughts and actions. It is to obey the axiom of Hermes:

Know yourself and you will know the universe and the gods

that was written in the temple *pronaos* (forecourt) to Apollo in Delphi. In the Gnostic system, you do not tell your misdeeds to a priest. When you fall into error, upon self-examination often you realize you were lying to yourself. As is so often the case, you discover through self-reflection that you have lost yourself in the confusion of angry politics, romantic intrigue, office gossip, stabbing other people in the back and are involved all kinds of irrational thinking. Therefore, the Gnostic, from time to time, asks himself or herself if he or she is walking the straight path of clear and positive thought. The Gnostic asks:

Have I been training my mind through the exercises of mind and positive thinking, or have I been lazy and allowed my precious mind to stagnate and rot?

You need to think clearly. You need to contact the center of your being that leads directly to the Center of the Universe, the Pleroma, the Heart of Light and Love in this galaxy!

What you're looking for is inside you.

explains Jesus in the Gnostic text the *Dialogue of the Savior*.

Lao-Tse, said:

Without stirring abroad, one can know the whole world; without looking out of the window one can see the way of heaven.

The inner power of life within you is the divine and the divine has all power. In *The Gospel According to Mary Magdalene*, it says:

Beware that no one lead you astray saying "lo here" or "lo there"! For the Child of True Humanity is within you. Follow after Him! Those who seek Him will find Him.

SIGNS THAT SOMEONE IS INFECTED WITH ALIEN PARASITES

Beware of arrogant people, people who show no respect for your personal boundaries and insult you (while smiling at you and pretending to be your friend), people who are always competing, arguing and debating with you, people who seek to demean, dominate, manipulate and control you, egotistical people, alcoholics, drug addicts, people who physically batter their spouses or abuse them with hurtful words, passive-aggressive people, liars and people who repeatedly say rude and abusive comments to you.

People infected with Alien Parasites use subtle intrusion tactics to implant their evil spawn into your mind. They use your own intention to be a good person and then turn that intention against you, changing you into a person who allows himself or herself to be victimized. It is healthy to be a person who seeks to be of help to his or her neighbor, but it is something else entirely (a sign of parasitic infection), to become a doormat for others to trample upon.

THE SECRET COSMIC BACK DOOR

The New Testament says in Matthew 6:22:

The lamp of the body is the eye. If therefore your eye is sound, your whole body will be full of light.

To perceive the Unity of the Divine is to perceive the Whole. Individuals have been given what is called a "back door" in computer programming. A back door is a software function programmed by the original designer (Creator) that will allow him or her to perform functions denied to normal users of the software. It is a secret way to enter the program. The Supreme Reality placed a back door throughout Existence.

In the Gnostic text *The Apocryphon of John* is written these magnificent words that describe the perfection of the Unique Reality:

For the perfection is majestic. He is pure, immeasurable mind. He is an aeon-giving aeon. He is life-giving life. He is a blessedness-giving blessed one. He is knowledge-giving knowledge. He is goodness-giving goodness. He is mercy and redemption-giving mercy. He is grace-giving grace, not because he possesses it, but because he gives the immeasurable, incomprehensible light.

Through this realization of the Unity of Reality, humanity can leap over and above all levels between those in the flesh and the

Pleroma! This is also known as the Reach of the Godhead. Herbert Christian Merillat wrote:

According to Gnostics, we must realize that there is at our core a spark of spirit which was once part of the universal spirit; that this individual spirit has become embedded in gross matter, in the body, through activities of lesser powers (often called archons or rulers), like the creator-lawgiver god of the Jews, who wishing to keep the human spirit in thrall; that we can escape this bodily prison by recognizing our true original home and evade the grasp of the archons and ascend again to that home — the spiritual Pleroma, the Fullness — to be reunited in Oneness. To put it another way, a human being can overcome the differentiation of this world, its dividedness into multiplicity and merge again into the primordial unity.

Certain people, such as Hermes Trismegistus and Enoch, could connect all the way up to Pleroma, bypassing all intermediaries. In *The Book of the Secrets of Enoch*, he travels through several heavens. Shamans, Sufis and others, regularly travel (ascend) up through various levels of intermediate beings. These levels stretch all the way from the planet Earth to the Pleroma. The Initiate Jesus was able to receive the Christos at the time of his Baptism. You have the power, through realizing the perfection of the spirit within you that is called Christic or the Christic Consciousness, to rise through all the levels of this hierarchy to the level of the Pleroma. In other words, you can transform from an existence as a mere computer simulation to experiencing a shared identity with the Absolute Reality. This is Gnosis: the casting off of all that is inauthentic and entering in all your nakedness into the waters of the Real Authenticity.

HUMANS HAVE CREATIVE POWER

J. Marvin Spiegelman has a Ph.D. from UCLA and is a Diplomate in clinical psychology, American Board of Professional Psychology. He is a graduate of the C. G. Jung Institute in Zurich, Switzerland and has taught at UCLA, USC and the Hebrew University in Jerusalem. He writes about the creative power of humanity in the following powerful passage:

The same power of imagination, which is world-creating in God, exists in man as even God-creating. This power of imagination (quwwat al-khal) makes possible our human potentialities for manifestation, inner and outer.

The computer games and digital special effects of today's media, as well as all works of art, music and literature, demonstrate that human beings have creative power. You are a free soul and therefore you must choose carefully what you think. Sometimes it is necessary to deny the evidence of your eyes, ears and senses. Continue to focus on what is beautiful and good, even while the whole world appears to be falling apart all around you. If you do this, you will find that, eventually, your outer world will match in experience with your inner thoughts and imagination.

PARANOIA AND DELUSION

A quick word must be said about paranoia and the fact that many psychologists would say that a belief in Alien Parasites is a delusion. The fields of psychology and psychiatry are battlegrounds where the war rages against the Archons and through which the Archons are fighting with all their weapons to destroy humanity. It is essential to know your own mind, its strengths and weaknesses. At the same time, there are many ignorant psychologists and psychiatrists who still believe in a material universe and are oblivious to spiritual reality.

The Archons have won great victories against humanity through controlling the minds of some psychologists and psychiatrists. 95% of the public will never understand the danger of Alien Parasites. Conspiracies have been occurring since the dawn of history and it is not paranoid to believe in conspiracies. Nor is it paranoid to believe in unseen beings and forces. If it is paranoid to believe in an unseen being, then all the people on Earth who believe in God would have to be diagnosed delusional by the psychiatric profession. The American physicist of Serbian origin, Nikola Tesla wrote:

"The day science begins to study non-physical phenomena, it will make more progress in one decade than in all the previous centuries of its existence."

While conspiracies have been well-documented as taking place throughout history, in every epoch and location, immediately when you begin to speak about the conspiracies that are happening now, you are labelled a "lunatic." This is because there exist very powerful, super-wealthy families with strong connections to the Demiurge who want to hide the fact that he is covertly taking control of Planet Earth.

A good counselor or therapist can help you a great deal. However, before you start working with them, talk and ask them what their beliefs are about conspiracies and extraterrestrials. Many therapists and counselors are very open-minded and have helped people to recover repressed memories about alien abductions. However, some psychologists and psychiatrists are, for the most part, brainwashed by the power-elite and are for that reason dangerous.

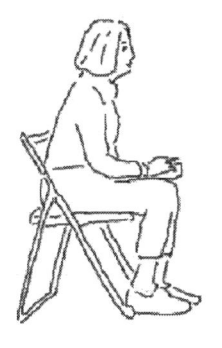

DIFFICULTY IN STUDYING GNOSTIC TEXTS

Most of the translators and commentators of the Nag Hammadi texts were and are people of Judeo-Christian and European origin. Therefore, they tend to consider Gnostic texts as a form of primitive Christianity. It is often difficult for the newcomer to understand traditional Gnostic writings. In many of the Nag Hammadi texts many words are missing due to the antiquity of the materials on which they were written. These leather-bound papyrus codices are around two-thousand years old, and have aged and crumbled and therefore it is not easy to decipher many sections and individual words. In addition, Gnosticism is essentially a Mystery Religion - a method of transmitting deep secrets about how to know God and the universe. The Gnostics used a form of code, a vocabulary and a language destined to be understood only by Initiates. Another difficulty with the Nag Hammadi Library is that the texts were written in a language called Coptic. They were originally written in another language, probably Greek. The problem with Coptic language is that it is a fabricated language, a kind of shorthand, which lacks subtleties. Most of the Gnostic texts were originally written by men, who by that time had begun to dominate the religions of the world. Therefore, reading these texts may be difficult for you and reading them might not convey to you the subtle secret teachings of the Gnostics. This author suggests that you begin a daily spiritual practice so that you can experience at a deep level the writings of these great wisdom teachers.

When the Nag Hammadi texts were first seen after nearly two thousand years, it was as if a time capsule was being opened. Humans could inhale for the first time the spiritual perfume of the times during which the first followers of Jesus walked the earth. These Gospels had been hidden for two millennia! However, when you read the four Gospels of the New Testament Bible, you are reading Gospels that have been edited, added and censored countless times over many centuries to fulfill the desires of powerful political and religious leaders. If an emperor or pope did not like a verse, it was removed. In addition, throughout the centuries, the scribe behind the scribe polished and enhanced the text to make the words more beautiful.

Most importantly, as times changed, so did the consciousness of humanity. Thus, the translations of these four Gospels changed with the times. The Catholic and Christian churches do not hide this fact. If you look at any popular Bible website, you can see several translations of the Bible, dating back to 1611 and earlier. Lately, it seems that a new translation is published every ten years. What is going on? The words of the Bible become acceptable, or normal, to the culture in which people live. The words of the *King James Bible* were normal to the culture of the people who lived at that time. The words of the *Contemporary English Version* are more appropriate to the culture of the people living in the present time. Some people consider the 1999 version to be the most normal and comfortable.

It is tempting to think that the problem is that people use different words nowadays. However, reality is much deeper than simple vocabulary. People of today think differently than their ancestors. Humanity is surrounded by a wall of scientific thought in the contemporary world. People believe that they control their own thoughts and that their thoughts are manufactured in their brains. People see the world with different eyes than the human beings who lived in the past. The consciousness of the Roman Empire was very different from the consciousness of the Age of Enlightenment and the consciousness of the Age of Enlightenment was very different from the consciousness of the First Industrial Revolution.

Since the time of the *Young's Literal Translation* in 1862, the world has become increasingly intellectual. Many people have replaced religion with scientism in Western culture. Scientists are the new priests. Another way of saying this is that humanity has become much more analytical and colder and less poetic and open-minded. Thus, when you open the "time capsule" of the Nag Hammadi Gospels, you experience Gospels that are exotic, uncommon and unknown to humanity. If humanity seeks to understand the unusual Gnostic Gospels, humanity must approach them with an equally unusual consciousness.

PART TWO: THE SOLUTION

ONE: PROTECTIVE SHIELD

Whenever you feel threatened by the Alien Parasites, immediately create a force field of electric blue light. The first step in this technique is to visualize the correct color of blue. This is the color blue that you sometimes see when a giant electric spark is emitted by some fallen electrical cable or electric power substation. If you cannot image this, light a snifter of brandy on fire in a dark room and observe the blue color of the flame. Finally, if all the above techniques do not help you to see this light in your mind's eye, you may visualize the blue color to be the tint of cobalt blue.

Second, you must set your intention. An "intention" is the exact purpose that this Electric Blue Shield of Protection will serve for you. In your own words, and always your own words are more potent than reading something pre-written for you by someone else, state that this Shield will protect you from all invasions of Alien Parasites, Evil Extraterrestrial Beings, demons, binding spells, curses, unwanted negative thought-forms, ancestral karma, physical attacks, astral attacks, (add whatever else you want to block); and then append to your intention that it is irrelevant whether or not the attacks come from your present time or any other time line, whether or not the attacks come from this dimension or any other dimension, and whether or not the attacks come from this world or from a parallel world or simulation.

Third, visualize yourself surrounded by this light. This light must be in the shape of a giant egg of light, extending at least one meter in all directions from your body. This is your Electric Blue Shield of Protection.

Fourth, visualize a brilliant star blazing above your head, inside the egg.

Fifth, in your mind's eye, imagine that this shining star explodes into a million tiny sparkling silver stars that twinkle and crackle with energy all around you while you are inside your Electric Shield of Protection.

This force field is a barrier of light, that if practiced (visualized regularly) will become an impenetrable barrier of light, keeping out all Alien Parasitical attacks. It is advisable to always do this practice before going to sleep, and whenever and wherever you feel that you are in any kind of danger.

TWO: STRENGTHEN YOUR MIND

Develop your intelligence. You need clear thinking to prevent an invasion of Alien Parasites, and to battle them. The "reality" of Las Vegas, Hollywood, *Haute Couture*, politics, pornography, advertising, supermarket tabloids, are all false realities designed to deceive and confuse you with what is truly authentic. They also weaken your mind, because these false realities hypnotize you. Your mind becomes weak and passive, and so therefore you have no mental defenses against the mind parasites. Strengthen your mind through puzzles, chess, continuing education classes, studying a foreign language, playing the ancient Chinese game called Go, and other games and tasks in which you must think calmly, clearly and on which you must focus all your attention. All this effort will protect you because these tasks and games are exercising your mind. The Christos declares in *The Gospel According to Mary Magdalene*:

For where the mind is there is the treasure.

It is so important to realize that Gnosticism is about an artificial reality and its collision with the real world. The artificial reality is the world of advertising, political propaganda, the degenerate society of materialism, addiction and so on. The goal is to leave the false creation and journey into the real world. All you need is one man or a woman to escape from the false world to bring a large group of people into the Light. Gnosticism is about liberation. The Kingdom of Heaven is a conscious faculty of seeing, hearing and comprehension. You have the power to reshape your reality.

THREE: NYMPHION

Make love to your spouse. The Archons cannot withstand the Light that envelops two people who love each other and who are making love. This light is called "The Perfect Light." It is a Gnostic sacrament. Alien Parasites cannot breach this protective aura or cell of light generated by the ritual of intercourse. The Greek term *Nymphion,* the "Bridal Chamber," was the codename for this protective shield of light. In the *Gospel of Philip*, it reads:

The powers do not see those who are clothed in the perfect light, and consequently are not able to detain them. One will clothe himself in this light sacramentally in the union.

However, do not confuse this sacred union with a counterfeit mockery of love begotten through a meaningless sexual act that solely serves to satisfy lustful desires. Friction is not love. To falsely join together with another person, or to mislead another person, in a participatory sacrament designed to manifest the Holy Androgynous Absolute and the first Human Being, is the greatest sacrilege of all. The *Nymphion* (Sacrament of the Bridal Chamber) is a ritual of love. To deliberately fake a sacramental union and thereby cause an artificial and inauthentic rift in the ritual, can bring upon you the most horrifying of Alien Parasitic experiences. To act thusly is consciously opening the door of your soul to demons. Nothing more foolish can be imagined. Likewise, do not get involved in romantic intrigues in which you are involved in several sexual relationships at the same time and feigning love with one or more of the persons with whom you are involved.

At times, it becomes necessary to leave an abusive spouse and unite with a new one who truly loves you. This is acceptable and healthy, for you must respect yourself. To continue to live or have sexual relations with someone who is abusing you and your children, is an invitation to the evil forces of the Alien Parasites to enter you and your family. The person who on a daily basis is struggling against Archontic manipulation is a person of integrity. The Huffington Post provides an excellent definition of integrity. They write:

Integrity stems from the Latin word 'integer' which means whole and complete. So, integrity requires an inner sense of 'wholeness' and consistency of character.

The Alien Parasites are trying to corrupt your concept of the Divine Feminine and the Divine Masculine. They are doing this by representing and encouraging a mockery of true androgyny in the public media and celebrity idols. Remember, the Archons want to confuse and corrupt you, they want to deform your sexuality. In some Gnostic Schools, it is said that some of the most exalted spirit beings are androgynous (having masculine and feminine qualities). However, the Gnostics explain that as the Absolute Reality progressively manifested Itself, the Absolute Reality disclosed Itself through two distinct genders and a transcendent child. The interplay of masculine and feminine have always been essential in Gnosticism. Clearly, when the Gnostics are referring to masculine and feminine energies, they are not speaking about men and women. Human beings did not manifest on the Earth until many outflows and emanations of the Divine had emerged and crystallized in the Solar System and on the Planet Earth. Even then, the division between men and women took eras to arise.

Carl Gustav Jung said, regarding the Assumption of the Virgin Mary, that she has already entered into the nuptial chamber and that thus, naturally, after a time there will be a child. This is communicated by Lewis Lafontaine in the Carl Jung Depth Psychology website, May 13, 2018, in his article: *Carl Jung on the "Assumption" – Anthology*. Lafontaine continues by stating, that Jung gave great importance to the Papal document of Pope Pius XII – 1950 – entitled the *Assumptio Maria*. Jung held that the written communication:

Points to the hieros gamos in the pleroma, and this in turn implies, as we have said, the future birth of the divine child, who, in accordance with the divine trend toward incarnation, will choose as his birthplace the empirical man. This metaphysical process is known as the individuation process in the psychology of the unconscious.

Liber Novus

It should be noted that the word 'man' was originally gender neutral, meaning more or less the same as the modern-day word "person". So then, according to Jungian psychology, "individuation" is the process of transforming one's psyche by bringing the personal and collective unconscious into consciousness.

As the great 20th century sage G. I. Gurdjieff or his mastermind student and confrere, P. D. Ouspensky, might put it, the mind is something like a mansion. Nevertheless, almost all of humanity is living in the basement of the mansion! Can you imagine that? What if you had a spectacular mansion, but only lived in the basement. Why would you ever do such a thing?

Once upon a time, a child was born to two parents who lived in the basement. Tragically, this occurred during the Great War, and the parents and family had to hide. The growing child had no idea about what was going on outside of her small world, only that her parents loved her and cared for her a great deal. She felt a great deal of security because her parents were a traditional couple, very dependable and the child had a stable routine. Daily life, while frightening for the girl's parents, was genuinely comforting for the girl. Kathryn Hatter, a veteran home-school educator, as well as a digital graphics creator and a regular contributor to Natural News wrote an article titled *How Lack of Stability Affects Children* on howtoadult.com:

Stability forms the backbone of a child's life, providing the structure, strength and consistency that supports the child emotionally and psychologically. If a child's life involves upset and unrest, due to any number of negative situations, the child is likely to suffer in different ways from a lack of stability.

Tragically, after a few years, both parents became ill with the terrible influenza that was sweeping the world at that time. Gradually, the young girl had to watch as her parents slowly became increasingly weaker with each day, and one especially sad morning, the young girl could not wake up her parents. The girl had never been taken upstairs to the mansion, because it was very dangerous during those times. However, the war ended, as all wars eventually due, with too much death and the real people in power continuing to earn their fortunes no matter which side won. Still, the now young adolescent had no idea about wars, or mansions, or hidden treasure.

Jung is telling you that the reason you do not take possession of your entire mansion, is that there is no communication between the basement and the upper floors. Sometimes due to certain circumstances such as the yarn above, people do not know that other areas of a building even exist and so it never occurs to them to attempt to contact that which they do not even know exists!

Metaphorically, you have never, or maybe only briefly or superficially, explored your basement. You have always assumed that the cellar is a dungeon with no value and probably very unsightly and probably dangerous. Therefore, you have carved out a small section of the basement, hung up some bedsheets so you will not see the rest of the cellar and into this tiny section of the cellar you have crammed a bed, a chair, a lamp, microwave, refrigerator and a few more necessities for survival. The tragic part of this story is that you never ventured forth from your self-imposed exile in your own home, to see what might be in the basement.

One day, you feel a new sense of courage pour into you. A rose-red sliver of shining light, wakes you up. You are not sure if you were dreaming this light, but now you are awake and you feel a deep need to have a look around. To your amazement, the basement is not at all as terrible as you imagined it to be. You discover some light switches, and when you turn them on, you discover that most of the basement at one time was a luxurious nightclub, perhaps from the time of prohibition. So, you begin exploring, and you feel a thrill of excitement as you feel a great yearning to know more about this place. It occurs to you that this is very much your home, as much as was that tiny corner in which you lived in the shadows for so many years.

As this is a sort of a fabulous fantasy, you can even imagine that you were under the impression that the only place that existed in the house was the basement. You felt safe there. Unfortunately, you had no idea what you were missing. You had heard rumors of upper floors, but you thought they were about as believable as the show you watched on your television about extraterrestrials visiting the earth in the past. Are your eyes deceiving you? Yet, there in front of you is something that is framed. It looks like it might be a map. You grab a cloth and wipe clean the glass, and you see a depiction of your basement. You see something that looks very much like a staircase. A large arrow points to the staircase. With the utmost caution you locate the staircase that was behind one of your curtains all this time, and you ascend to see your first floor for the first time in your life! The sunlight is blinding, and you quickly hide behind some furniture because the light is painful. Then bit by bit, you notice that your eyes are somehow adjusting to this new kind of light, and you are able to make out various objects in the spacious living area.

Now, you are finally aware that you were not condemned to live your life in a tiny little room. You have now discovered that you have a beautiful basement and an expansive first floor. With renewed courage, you return to the basement. After much rummaging around you discover some old-fashioned "Steamer Trunks" (gigantic luggage that the wealthy utilized when traveling the world during their ocean cruises). To use this type of luggage, you stand the "Steamer Trunk" up on its end and open it to reveal separated compartments on each side. You have seen movies from the 1930s and 1940s and with just a little work you manage to open the trunks.

To your astonishment, these giant trunks contain all manner of treasures.

Jungian analyst Anthony Stevens writes in "Private Myths: Dreams and Dreaming":

Individuation is the process, simple or complex as the case may be, by which every living organism becomes what it was destined to become from the beginning.

Jung is attempting to communicate that you can no longer hide your most secret wishes in your unconscious. The Nymphion is a technique by which you can invite your subconscious to visit you and introduce itself. This book uses the more familiar word "subconscious" as it would require a separate book to explain the "unconscious." Mirriam-Webster on their website, helps to define the term "subconscious" as it is used in this book:

We're rarely aware, or at least fully aware, of our subconscious mental activity. But subconscious thought does affect our feelings and behavior, and it's often revealed in dreams, artistic expression and slips of the tongue. The subconscious mind can be a hiding place for anxiety, a source of creativity and often the reason behind our own mysterious behavior.

You must become aware of all that lives inside that part of your mind. Eastern sages have taught about the Yin-Yang symbol. The image consists of a circle divided into two teardrop-shaped halves—one white and the other black. In Chinese philosophy, Yin and Yang is a concept of dualism in ancient Chinese philosophy. The Yin-Yang symbol represents according to Roger Jahnke, author of *The Healing Power of Qi*, not just Yin and Yang, but also their constant interaction and essentially, "tells the whole story of the universe in one image."

Mistakenly, many people confuse duality with polarity. In spiritual growth it is important to focus on polarity. Polarity can be viewed as complimentary forces that work together to create balance, on the other hand, duality is the belief in opposing forces that conflict with each other and create chaos. Your goal is to establish a balance between the two poles. In duality one is "better" or "above" another, and this is responsible for so much suffering on the Planet. Some people believe they are more worthy, more deserving than others and they take far more than they need. People compare themselves to others and judge themselves as being "better" or "worse", which leads to an inflated ego or hating oneself. If you really want peace in your life, this author recommends letting go of duality altogether.

Where duality divides things into black or white, polarity includes the full spectrum, it is all inclusive. Duality takes the spectrum and draws a line somewhere, cutting it in half. Duality really only exists in the mind; it does not directly relate to the physical realm. Duality attempts to create "contradictory opposites," such as: dark-light and old-young. For a moment, consider the concepts of dark and light. The English language has such terms as: dawn, dusk, first light, daybreak, twilight, crepuscule and evenfall. Yet, not one of these terms outlines an absolute demarcation point between dark and light. You may consider other issues and themes that the public, or even spiritual groups, want to split down the middle in a dualistic manner.

With polarity you can see that there are various degrees in between what are often considered "fixed" sounds, colors, emotional reactions and even subjects such as wealth and poverty. In many "New Age" groups, much emphasis is placed upon "vibration," "frequency," "levels of spiritual evolution", "planes of existence", and "dimensions". This author's first book began by addressing this very subject. For a moment, think of a symphony orchestra. In your mind's eye, visualize that you are seated in the best seat of the house. Now, imagine the lights dim, the conductor takes the podium and the music begins. You first hear the double-bass playing a deep and profound note that reaches deep inside you. Then consider the violinist playing a sweet and soothing high note. You, the reader of this book, know that there is an entire spectrum of musical frequencies. The instruments that produce the low notes, produce very slow frequencies. Likewise, the instruments that play the high notes, produce very rapidly oscillating frequencies. You cannot say that the bass player is producing music that is of a very low spiritual frequency. Many "experts" will tell you that 1st Density is the lowest density, corresponding to subatomic particles, atoms, molecules, chemicals, and minerals; while the 4th Density includes beings that straddle the boundary between space-time and the higher ethereal realms. An orchestra needs every instrument of the orchestra in order to make it a true orchestra. An orchestral symphony or violin concerto, needs all the vibrations in that musical spectrum (including some that cannot be heard, but only "felt").

What is the best way to confuse a person? Have him or her doubt his or her sexuality. Equally absurd are the correspondingly diabolical attempts of the Archons to create exaggerated male and female role models and archetypes for the public to adore. Too many men think that having huge muscles and becoming dominant and egotistical makes them men, and hence pre-eminent over women. Jung mentioned this condition as follows:

The most masculine man needs women, and he is consequently their slave.

The exaggerated concept of the sexes, too, is a lie of the Archons. Many women think that starving to death, looking like a popular doll, and losing their own respect makes them women. A supposed general physical ideal, for both sexes, still is embedded in the public's heads, and thanks to the media and technology (the playground of the Inauthentic Agenda), it is even harder to block out than it used to be. According to a study in *Pediatrics*, about two-thirds of girls in the 5th to 12th grades said that magazine images influence their vision of an ideal body, and about half of the girls said the images made them want to lose weight. Again, the Archons through their manipulation of the media (in this case magazines) attack the female human population, causing young women untold distress and self-hatred – the food of the Archons.

Gnosticism is a path in which you learn to respect both aspects of your being: the feminine and the masculine, and to profoundly learn from these qualities. C.G. Jung taught about two forces which he named the *animus* and the *anima*. Jung described the animus as the unconscious masculine side of a woman, and the anima as the unconscious feminine side of a man, with each transcending the personal psyche. The goal of the person, in reaching individuation and having a whole personality is to integrate the side opposite to their gender. The goal is not to change their sex or sexual orientation; the goal is to integrate the masculine and feminine forces. Homophobia in the male would be an example of a person desperate to overpower and extinguish aspects of himself that he thinks are feminine. Jung did not suggest that by accessing the feminine side one becomes a homosexual, if one is a man. Rather he reaches out to receive the gifts normally ascribed to the anima and the sacred feminine. The ability to emotionally relate to others, the creative force and hence the artistic force are *anima* characteristics. A man who is creative, a great listener and has successful relationships is likely to be in touch with his anima.

For women, accessing the masculine side, or *animus*, gives women the ability to use reason, think along logical terms and assert physical strength and intellect, among many other masculine traits. The idea of being brave and being strong are more commonly thought of as masculine attributes.

To Jung it is the rejection of *anima* and *animus* that leads many people to have significant psychological problems. The Gnostics teach the Sacred Union of the Divine Feminine and Divine

Masculine. Love and respect your body. Do not let yourself fall under the influence of the Hollywood and Social Media representations of the perfect man or woman. Hollywood and the internet are filled with men and women completely possessed by Archons. They are not looking out for your welfare; they are looking to destroy you.

FOUR: SOUND REINFORCEMENT AND MOTIVATION

Was music once a proof of God's existence?

Seamus Heaney

Sing beautiful songs. Play great music downloads on your mp3, cellular phone, radio, computer, or cable television. Learn to play a musical instrument. When you listen to music, it releases the hormone dopamine into the brain. Researchers at McGill University in Montreal said the dopamine was released at moments of maximum enjoyment of a song or musical composition, for example when you are listening to music and you experience chills and shivers down your spine. Dopamine is a common neurotransmitter in the brain. It is released in response to rewarding human activity and is related to reinforcement and motivation - these include activities that are biologically significant such as eating and sex. In a McGill study, dopamine levels were found to be up to 9% higher when volunteers were listening to music they enjoyed.

Michael Friedman Ph.D., of *Psychology Today* writes:

We now know through controlled treatment outcome studies that listening to and playing music is a potent treatment for mental health issues. Research demonstrates that adding music therapy to treatment improves symptoms and social functioning . . . music therapy has demonstrated efficacy as an independent treatment for reducing depression, anxiety and chronic pain.

In addition, many Gnostics used chanting and singing of vowels and special names in order to open specific spiritual gateways (portals) thereby achieving ecstatic states of consciousness. True Gnostics do not learn Gnosis from a book; rather the Supreme One Reality fills the Gnostic with Gnosis. In the book, *The Discourse on the Eighth and Ninth*, one of the *Hermetic* books from the Nag Hammadi Library, there are hymns with names and vowels intended to be intoned. Hermetic signifies anything pertaining to Hermes Trismegistus, or to theosophy, and later alchemy and astrology. Hermes Trismegistus may be associated with the Greek god Hermes and the Egyptian god Thoth. Some of the hymns with names and vowels in *The Discourse on the Eighth and Ninth*, such as have been deciphered are:

ΖΩΞΑΘΑΖΩ

Α ΩΩ

ΕΕ ΩΩΩ

ΗΗΗ ΩΩΩΩ

ΗΗ ΩΩΩΩΩΩ

ΟΟΟΟΟ ΩΩΩΩΩΩ

YYYYY ΩΩΩΩΩΩΩΩΩΩΩΩΩΩ

ZΩZAZΩΘ

and:

ZŌKSATHAZŌ

A ŌŌ

EE ŌŌŌ

ĒĒĒ ŌŌŌŌ

ĒĒ ŌŌŌŌŌŌ

OOOOO ŌŌŌŌŌŌ

UUUUU ŌŌŌŌŌŌŌŌŌŌŌŌŌ

ZŌZAZŌTH

These are probably not precisely the correct names and vowels to say, as the text is ancient. While the text is probably no longer exactly accurate, it gives the reader an idea of the sorts of sounds the Gnostics did make during their ceremonies. Regrettably, many modern Gnostics place too much evidence on analysis and not enough on praxis (practice or discipline for a specific purpose). Praxis is the practical application of any branch of learning.

Jonathan Goldman is an American author, musician and teacher in the fields of Harmonics and Sound Healing. In Jonathan Goldman's magnificent book Healing Sounds: *The Power of Harmonics*, he writes:

William Grey, one of the greatest Western magicians of this century, writes of vowels in "The Talking Tree." The chanting of the particular vowel sounds has the ability of connecting the chanter with the energies of the Divine. Through chanting the vowel sounds keyed by what Grey called "The Master-Code of the "Word" A.E.I.O.U., one could effect a 'fully cosmated consciousness.' Each of the vowel sounds chanted in specific combinations could create resonance with particular divine aspects.

[*"Cosmates" a term invented by Empedocles, means "intergalactic cosmic rays that travel faster than the speed of light."]

Jonathan Goldman also mentions William G. Gray (1913-1992), in the above quote. William G. Gray, better known to many as Bill Gray, was an English ceremonial magician, Hermetic Kabbalist and writer, who published widely on the subject of western esotericism and the occult. Gray founded a magical order known as the *Sangreal Sodality*.

Consequently, this book suggests that the reader begin a regular daily practice of chanting the vowels. It is well-worth the time and effort to obtain Goldman's opus if you are interested in more deeply exploring this potent means to contact the Gods and Goddesses.

It would not be surprising if the vocalized sounds from the time of *The Discourse on the Eighth and Ninth* were not accompanied by particular drum rhythms, as well sacred movements (dancing). In the Gnostic path of Sufism which goes back to the 7th century CE, the practitioners regularly chant divine names, which rely heavily on vowel sounds, such as: HU, HAYY and LA ILAHA ILLA'LLAH, as they whirl, sway and sing to the accompaniment of shamanic drumming. The Sufis also make extensive use of vocal overtones (changing the sound of the words being chanted by subtle and overt changes of the breath and shape of the mouth, tongue and throat). The author is convinced beyond any shadow of a doubt, that these Sufi practices were influenced by much earlier shamanic and hermetic practices, as the author has substantial practice and study in both fields. The author suggests that the reader who desires to explore the spiritual mysteries of the vowels, begin his or her exploration of the mysteries of sound by chanting one vowel per day and then sitting in silence while quietly observing the effect of the vowel on the physical and spiritual bodies.

Larkfall in the article "Say Aaah: Music of the Vowels" posted in "Arcana, Music and Theory, XETB" writes:

The idea that the vowels hold the secret to some mystical, primal language appears to have a genuinely ancient lineage. Notably they seem bound up with the ritual expressions of the Gnostics. For example, in the Nag Hammadi codices we find a Hermetic dialogue entitled The Discourse on the Eighth and Ninth. As in some of the dialogues of the Corpus Hermeticum (XI & XIII), the master in this dialogue also breaks from philosophical and theological speculations to sing: as though poetry, sound and music may provide the pupil with another route to divine experience alongside meditation and philosophical instruction.

It is said that before humankind spoke any language, humans used a song-like means to communicate that emphasized the use of vowels. This was called the *Language of the Birds*. In mythology, medieval literature and occultism, the *Language of the Birds* is postulated as a mystical, perfect divine language, or *green* language.

Learning to play a musical instrument is an instance of an individual intensifying his or her relationship with the surrounding environment. The Gnostic has a foot in each world. They bridge the threshold. Gnostics are the liminal people. As Plato said:

Music and rhythm find their way into the secret places of the soul.

FIVE: PRAYERS

Say special prayers to the Aeons, Christos, Sophia, the Initiate Jesus, your guardian angel, archangels, saints, the Pleroma and directly to the Unknown Mystery.

Some examples from the *Gnostic Prayerbook: Rites, Rituals, Prayers and Devotions* by J. Puma are:

O Most Holy Christos and Sophia, be with me and watch over me as I go about my day. I give thanks to you for another opportunity to serve others and in so doing serve you.

Dearest Sophia, we pray that you may rekindle the divine spark within all your poor children of the Light, that the Logos may lift them into the limitless joy and brilliance of the Pleroma.

Unknown Mystery who dwells above the Pleroma, we honor your holy Names. May your Aeons unfold over the World, and may your work be accomplished within the World as it is accomplished in the Pleroma.

I stand before the Christos and Sophia as a seeker of Gnosis. I will seek to come to know myself.

I renounce the Archon, his works and his deeds.

I will live my life to the best of my ability, seeking Gnosis wherever it may be found.

In the Gnostic *Codex Brucianus* there survives this fragment of a Gnostic hymn:

Hear me as I sing praises to thee, O Mystery who existed before every incomprehensible one and every endless one. Hear me as I sing praises to thee, O Mystery, who hast shone in thy mystery, so that the mystery which exists from the beginning should be completed.

Another beautiful prayer, written by Ernest Holmes, that you can recite is:

All the power that there is and all the presence that there is and all the life that there is, is God - the all-powerful living spirit - and this living Divine Spirit is within me.

SIX: AFFIRMATIONS

Say the following affirmation upon awakening and then several times throughout the day:

I am Christos-Sophia, the divine living couple within me. The Pleroma overflows, filling me with divine love, intelligence and power. I come from the Pleroma. Divine Intelligence made me. This Divine Mind is my mind. This Perfect Intelligence cannot experience a state of delusion. My thoughts are clear and rational. My thought is the divine thought. I am free from doubt and confusion. I am greater than all Alien Parasites. I am directly connected to the Divine Source. My origin is in the Imperishable Realm. I am more powerful than the alien parasites of chaos. I have an unlimited supply of courage. The One Infinite Life of the Pleroma is my life now. I erase from my consciousness the belief that anything (or any being) can interfere, impair, or harm the One Infinite Life and Substance. My mind is maintained by the All-Powerful Essence of the Pleroma. I am in the loving arms of Christos-Sophia. Nothing can flourish unless there is something to nourish it. Therefore, my thought does not sustain false ideas because I do not think negative, painful and disturbing thoughts. I focus my mind like a laser beam on what is noble, inspiring, loving, joyful and beautiful. The All-Powerful Mind of the Indwelling Christos-Sophia in me dissolves all belief in fear, anxiety, depression and delusion. My Highest Self dwells in the Pleroma now and forever!

SEVEN: NATURE

Dance to your favorite songs. Paint beautiful pictures. Place magnificent quotes, photos and stunning images of nature scenes on your walls. Studies have proven that even photos of nature, if you cannot observe or visit a natural setting easily, will cause your mind to feel calm and peaceful. You can economically print a color photocopy of your photo file at an Internet Café. Place it near the entrance to your home, so that whenever you enter, it is the first thing you see. In *The Gospel According to Mary Magdalene*, the Christos says:

Be of good courage, and if you are discouraged be encouraged in the presence of the different forms of nature.

These are especially amazing words coming from the Christos, because during the time during which the Gnostic Gospels were written, people took very little notice of nature in the sense of nature being someplace one visited to gain spiritual inspiration. Nature was a place of testing; for example, when the Christos went into the Judaean Desert to fast for forty days and forty nights immediately after the Baptism. Nature was where many people earned their daily bread, for example through farming and animal husbandry. Nature was merely the daily backdrop of people's lives. The idea of nature being a place to visit for its own sake did not begin to appear until rather recently in history.

EIGHT: AROMA

Therefore, the incense of life is in me.

Gospel of the Egyptians

Burn aromatic incense. This author recommends the following incense to clear your mind of Alien Parasites: pine, sandalwood, sage, *palo santo*, lavender, jasmine, lemon, magnolia, myrrh, thyme, ylang-ylang and copal. Used to aromatize and create an harmonious environment, these aromas have been the protagonists of various religions and cultures since the Ancient Age, and can be of great help in meditation and contact with the spiritual world.

Ritual offering by Jesus of the incense of the mystery for taking away the evil of the Archons, sealing of the disciples with a seal.

Books of Jeu Book 2

NINE: SELF-OBSERVATION

Become aware of your body. Feel each and every part. Begin by becoming aware of your feet, and then your ankles, up your shins and calves, then your knees and thighs, following by your buttocks and genitals. Continue becoming increasingly aware of your lower back, and then middle back, your lower abdomen and then upper abdomen. Proceed up to your upper back and shoulders, and then become conscious of your chest. Move to your hands, as you familiarize yourself with the sensations in your fingers, palms, wrists, lower arms, elbows, and upper arms. Continue by sensing your throat and the back of your neck. Finally, become aware of the back of your head, the top of your head, your forehead, eyes, nose, cheeks, lips and jaw. Do all of this slowly, relaxing deeply as you become aware of each part of your body. If you come to a section of your body and you do not feel any sensation or feeling in that area, pause, relax, and wait until you truly sense that part of the body.

At that moment, add to your full physical body awareness an awareness of your emotions. How do you feel? Happy, sad, bored, enthusiastic, nervous, exalted, lonely, inquisitive, fearful, angry, joyous, upset, indignant, astonished, proud, loving? Recognize how you feel right now. At this point in the exercise, you are aware of both your physical body and your emotions.

Continue to expand your field of observation and tell yourself if you are thinking of anything at this time. Are you thinking negative thoughts like: I am not good enough; I cannot do it; I am not lucky like other people; I am not strong enough; nobody cares; I am out of control; I am weak; I am defective; or are you thinking about financial matters, your job, your boyfriend or girlfriend, husband or wife, or the latest news in the world of politics? Do *not* judge your body, feelings and thoughts. Just be aware of them. To the degree that you can, do not entertain your thoughts. Allow your mind to quiet itself on its own. Simply notice what is happening inside of you. If you have a thought, think of it as just a cloud drifting by, and notice as it comes and goes. Do not engage in a struggle with distractions. Pay attention. Continue to be aware. Do not play with the mind, for it will continuously generate all sorts of thoughts. It is like a little puppy trying to get your attention. Just relax and let the thoughts drift away.

Lastly, see yourself as if you were another person who is now looking at you, wherever you are. You might be sitting in a room by yourself. See this person (yourself) sitting in a chair in the room. Observe yourself and your surroundings very carefully. Try to do this self-observation all the time. Take notice of that which you call "you." In a relaxed and detached way, explore what arises when you think "I am." Become acquainted with yourself. Ask yourself, "Who am I?"

At times, you will not have the opportunity to do the first part of this exercise in which you place your awareness at each part of your body. For example, you may be in conversation with a group of people. This is perfectly all right. Just observe yourself, as if you were an impartial observer watching yourself in conversation with other people.

Be aware of your totality. Feel your consciousness expanding. Try to sense that your consciousness extends outward beyond your physical body. Realize that your consciousness continues at least several inches away from your physical form. Practice this self-observation exercise many times a day. Challenge yourself to see how many seconds, minutes and even hours you can continue self-observation without interruption. Note: It is more challenging to self-observe when you are angry or having an argument with someone. When you realize and observe yourself, you are placing an especially powerful protective shield around you that protects you from Alien Parasites. The last power that an Archon wants you to manifest is the power of awareness. The aware person is the person who can see through lies, deception and manipulation. The more aware you are, the greater the chance you have of discovering the reason that you are angry or arguing, and the greater the chance you have of re-establishing your serenity. You are of no use to Archontic forces if you are an aware person. Even worse, for their point of view, you establish yourself as a potent warrior capable of cutting off the Archons supply of human life energy.

TEN: THE DIVINE FACE

Find a painting or reproduction of Christ Jesus and place it in your home and office. [Do not use any depiction of the Passion or Crucifixion. Nevertheless, the Shroud of Turin is acceptable as it depicts the moment of Resurrection.]

On October 27, 1845, the Christos said to Sister Marie de Saint-Pierre:

By My Holy Face you shall work wonders.

Sister Marie herself said:

Our Lord has promised me that He will imprint His Divine likeness on the souls of those who honor His Holy Countenance.

These are wonderful promises. If you are suffering from Alien Parasites and consciously meditate on the divine face, this meditation will erase all traces of the parasites and replace them with the original divine template of your being. This act is similar to erasing the hard drive of a computer that has a virus and resetting it to the original factory specifications.

The mind reset accomplished through the Divine Likeness is a natural method that works not only with a human being's physical brain, but also with a person's Physical, Etheric and Astral Bodies. *The Etheric Body* is the natural blueprint of the body and contains all the information necessary for the proper growth and maintenance of the Physical Body. The *Astral Body* contains all human emotions. As was an image of the instant of the Resurrection emblazoned upon the Shroud of Turin, so too an image of the Divine Likeness is imprinted upon your soul (which in esotericism is called the Astral Body) when you view the face on the shroud. However, any image that you prefer of the Christos is acceptable for this practice. The image of the Christos purifies your Astral Body, which when purified is called in some spiritual Gnostic systems — *Sophia*. In other words, through contemplation on the Holy Face, a *catharsis* occurs. The Cambridge English Dictionary defines katharsis as: the process of releasing strong emotions through a particular activity or experience, such as writing or theatre, in a way that helps you to understand those emotions. This katharsis creates inner organs of perception (the supersensible organs that can see and perceive the spiritual).

To be more specific, Sophia (Astral Body), having now developed inner organs of perception, permeates the Etheric and Physical Bodies and imprints an image of its "inner organs of perception" upon both these inner "bodies." At this point, when Sophia becomes aware the Divine, it then can receive the Beloved, the Christos. One may also say Sophia becomes aware of the cosmic and universal Absolute Reality. The individual is filled and surrounded with spiritual light. At this moment, the human being attains illumination (also known as *photismos*).

A SPECIAL NOTE ON THE GNOSTIC TEACHINGS OF THE CRUCIFIXION

Gnostics do not encourage suffering in any way. As has been alluded to earlier in this book, there have been many Gnostic "schools" (spiritual points of view regarding Gnosticism, several of which were founded by a charismatic leader). For example, a great many Gnostics do not believe that the Christos suffered and died on the cross. Others believe that the Christos concluded his work while on the cross and at that time returned control of the Physical, Etheric and Astral Bodies back to the Initiate Jesus. And finally, a third teaching holds that neither the Christos, nor the Initiate Jesus, suffered, died and was buried.

If you personally were brought up to believe that Christ Jesus suffered and died for you, then you must recognize that the debt has already been paid and you owe nothing. For example, if you owed a great amount of money on your bank credit card and someone went to your bank and paid your debt in full, your debt would be paid. It is said that Jesus died for the sin of Adam, and hence, for the sins of humankind. Many Catholic, Protestant and Evangelical preachers say that, in order to benefit from Christ Jesus' sacrifice, you must accept Him as your Lord and Savior. However, pause and do the following thought experiment: if someone pays your credit card debt, then you do not need to recognize that person in any special way to receive the benefits of what that person did for you. You do not need to call him or her your friend. You do not even need to know who it was that paid your debt in order to benefit from his or her generosity. In the eyes of your bank, your debt is paid in full. You will not have to go to court and stand in front of a judge and account for your debt, and you will no longer be in debt. No further activity is needed on your part. To paraphrase what the Christos might say to you if you believe that He suffered, died and was resurrected to pay the price for your sins, then you might imagine the Christos saying to you the following words:

Why are you continuing to suffer in my Name, when I have already suffered? Are you so arrogant to think that my suffering was incomplete and not sufficient? Why do you continue to idolize suffering as if it were the goal and purpose of my coming to Earth? I already suffered for you, so you could be free. You owe me nothing. What I did on the cross, I did of my own Free Will. You are insulting me if you believe I need you to suffer, crawl on your knees, pray for hours on end and live your life feeling guilty!

The idea of false renunciation (self-sacrifice) is not contained in the teachings of the Christos. This idea of renunciation was created by the Roman Catholic Church which was hungry for money and power. It is truly the time to eliminate all images of the suffering Christ: bloody and beaten, weak and tortured. These images are designed to fill the Catholic with tremendous feelings of guilt; the horrible misconception that because of their sins Christ Jesus had to suffer such nightmarish torture and death. Nothing more diabolical, nor more evil, can be imagined than filling the hearts and minds of young people with guilt that will live inside of them for the rest of their lives! The Christos came to Earth to teach you about your potential, to be the first of many, helping every man and woman to become a "Christ." To place the focus on Golgotha is to truly place your focus on "The Place of the Skull."

In several Gnostic texts, the Christos refers to the events that occurred at the site called Calvary, which in Hebrew is called Golgotha, a hill that resembles a skull located near the walls of Jerusalem.

In the *First Apocalypse of James*, the Christos comforts James by saying:

Never have I suffered in any way, nor have I been distressed. And this people has done me no harm.

In the *Second Treatise of the Great Seth*, the Christos says:

I did not die in reality but in appearance.

According to some Gnostics, the Christos completed his work when he was crucified. At that moment, the Christos left the Initiate Jesus. There is evidence that Jesus survived the crucifixion and afterward married Mary Magdalene and that they had a child together by the name of Sarah.

It is quite possible that Barabbas was the crucified person. The name Barabbas means "Son of the Father." In *John 10: 29-30* you can read:

"My Father who has given them to me is greater than all. No one is able to snatch them out of my Father's hand. I and the Father are one."

Then you learn that there were two men named Jesus:

They had then a notable prisoner called Jesus Barabbas. When therefore they were gathered together, Pilate said to them, "Whom do you want me to release to you? Jesus Barabbas, or Jesus who is called Christ?"

Matthew 27: 16-17

"Barabbas" (or "Bar Abbas") is the Hellenized form of the Aramaic name Bar Abba, which means "Son of the Father". And the name "Jesus" (from the Greek "Yesous") is the Hellenized form of the Hebrew name Yeshua. Pilate was essentially asking the Jerusalem crowd:

Who do you want me to release: Yeshua son of the Father or Yeshua son of the Father whom your followers call Messiah?

The fact that both men had the same name has been covered up by Catholic and Christian churches, but it is obvious that there was a great opportunity for confusion during this highly emotional, chaotic and devised moment.

Adepts and saints have such a deep and ecstatic connection to the Divine that they are not aware of any physical suffering while being martyred. There are Gnostics who believe in the Resurrection. Rudolf Steiner, the famous Christian Gnostic, taught that the blood of the Christos had to enter the Earth. As the Christos is the consort of Sophia and Sophia is the Earth, the mixture of the blood of the Christos with the body of Sophia, is the ritual called in the Greek *Hierogamia* (Sacred Marriage). Plainly speaking, the crucifixion then becomes a symbolic sexual relationship between the Christos and Sophia.

In the *Secret Book of James*, the disciples still have a conversation with Jesus more than eighteen months after He had risen from the grave. *Pistis Sophia*, meanwhile states that He spent eleven years with His followers after the resurrection.

The Christos did not need to die for the sins of humankind. The Absolute Reality is perfectly capable of forgiving humanity without requiring the death of anyone and even less of his own Son. Miguel

Conner, in his article "How Did the Gnostics View the Crucifixion of Jesus?" writes:

Despite the varied beliefs in Gnosticism, there is a common thread on most versions of the Passion narrative: The Savior arrives in a form recognizable to humans; his form is destroyed by the demonic agents that rule the universe (the blame is never on the Jews or Romans); and lastly he returns in an astral manifestation to impart his greatest teachings to those who both had faith and understood his message from the beginning.

The Initiated Adept Jesus could revivify his own flesh through his Christic Body of Pure Light and become the Fully-Actuated "new creation." The lesson to be learned is that you too can receive the Christos and become illumined. The Christos is the Divine Seed and Sophia is the Sacred Fertile Land. Your task is to prepare the land (Physical, Etheric and Astral, bodies) to receive the Spirit of the Christos, and thus the land will flourish again. The Christos calls you to awake out of sleep. He spoke plainly about the true nature of the Absolute Reality:

He is not the God of the dead, but the God of the living.

Mark 12:27

With regard to the subject of crucifixion and resurrection, it is advisable to practice an ancient Gnostic exercise. Train yourself to keep two completely contradictory ideas within your heart and head. The eminent visionary, David Icke, states:

It is important to realize that two contradictory statements may be equally true depending on the level at which the same situation is observed.

As you develop into the "Completely Updated Human Being," you will gradually begin to understand the events that took place two thousand years ago on Golgotha.

ELEVEN: POSITIVE FRAME OF MIND

Strive to achieve a positive frame of mind. Cultivate thinking in a positive way. Every day read inspirational books and articles by authors such as Eckhart Tolle, Clarissa Pinkola Estés, Tobias Churton, Carlos Cuauhtémoc Sánchez, Leonard Jacobson, Myrtle Fillmore, Jorge Luis Borges, Robert A. Heinlein, Mike Dooley, Gangaji, Ernest Holmes, Neville Goddard, Kahlil Gibran, Melody Beattie, C. S. Lewis, Jack Canfield, Jane Roberts, Neal Donald Walsch, Helena Blavatsky, Gregg Braden, Terry Cole-Whittaker, Napoleon Hill, Richard Smoley, Rudolf Steiner, Marcus Aurelius, Rabindranath Tagore, Gary Lachman, Carlos Castañeda, Terence McKenna, Joel S. Goldsmith, Ralph Waldo Emerson, June Singer, Paramahansa Yogananda, Jeff Kripal, Esther Hicks, Miguel Conner, Shakti Gawain, Richard Bach, Tony Robbins, Douglas Gabriel, John Munter, Laurence Caruana, Tyla Gabriel, Wallace Wattles, Maxwell Maltz, Amelia Bert, Louise Hay, Jeremy Puma, Max Heindel and the like. Attend church or a spiritual group regularly. Watch inspirational and uplifting movies and videos.

Remember to include humor in your life. Laughter is mandatory. Too often spiritual explorers become laden down with so many ponderous thoughts that they forget to laugh and have fun. While you may never have thought about this lack of laughter in your life, in reality this is a serious problem from which many creative, intelligent and spiritual people suffer. Look around your home and perhaps you will notice that you do not own one object that is silly, frivolous and maybe even outright funny. Well, it is time to change that situation in your home. Along with furnishing your home with some comical and amusing items, include reading matter in your effort to bring joviality into your life: reading funny novels, comic magazines and articles that you find absolutely hilarious. Be cautious here not to allow political humor, or humor at anyone's expense, to subtly poison your moments of joyfulness. Some excellent authors that will bring a smile to your face are: Douglas Adams, P.G. Wodehouse, Woody Allen, Steve Martin, Terry Pratchett and John Kennedy Toole. Perform an internet search for the top thirty comedy novels of all time – there is sure to be one book in the list that will tickle your funny bone.

Essential to maintaining a positive frame of mind is a proper beginning to your day. Start your day with deep breathing exercises, sungazing, meditation, affirmations, devotional prayer, an invigorating shower, or whatever particular ritual you may invent on your own. After all, Gnosticism is a path that you must create and tailor for yourself. You can borrow and utilize the thoughts, inspirations and examples of other human beings, but at the end of the day, you are unique and the path you tread must be your own.

TWELVE: PURIFICATION

The apostles said to the disciples, "May our entire offering obtain salt." They called Sophia "salt". Without it, no offering is acceptable.

Gospel of Philip

Cross the water to avoid evil. If you feel you are being pursued by the Archons, try crossing a stream, river or lake. To remove Alien Parasites, take frequent showers and baths. Always look for running water; never use standing water. Regularly splash water on your face, hands and feet. Shower outside in the rain. Salt water is the best purifier. Immerse yourself in the ocean. If this is not possible, put a little sea salt in a bucket of water and pour it over your head and body while you are in the shower. All sources of fresh running water are also very useful in eliminating Alien Parasites.

Additionally, be cautious about water (and other beverages) served at restaurants and parties. Do not leave your glass of water (or beverage) alone and unobserved at any time. Ask a trusted friend to watch your glass for you if you need to leave the room.

Salt plays a special role in purifying and absorbing negativity in your living space. Obtain some sea salt and sprinkle it in all the corners of your home, moving in a clockwise direction as you scatter the salt around each corner of every room. Also, place the sea salt across the threshold to your home.

Other methods to maintain positive energies in your home: purchase a fountain, light a white candle, play soothing music, open the windows and allow the fresh air and sunshine to enter, throw out garbage, regularly clean your living space, create a place for your shoes at the entrance of your home and walk barefoot or in slippers, place many plants and cacti around your abode, remove photos of people and places that are painful or sad for you to see and very importantly: reduce as much as possible electro-magnetic pollution.

The Sufis (ostensibly Islamic mystics, but in reality a group whose roots reach back thousands of years throughout Eastern Asia) teach that salt symbolizes purity and incorruptibility. Salt was an essential step in the mummification process of the ancient Egyptians.

THIRTEEN: THE POWER OF FLOWERS AND CACTI

Always have fresh flowers in your home. Inhale their beautiful fragrance. Be uplifted by their beautiful shapes and scents. Consider hanging flower baskets if space is at a premium for you in your dwelling space. If you cannot afford to purchase flowers or plants, there are always beautiful wildflowers and plants that grow on the side of the road that you can pick and bring home with you. The beauty and aroma of plants and flowers draws you closer to the Goddess Sophia. Thus, plants and flowers help to connect you to the Divine.

In *Feng Shui* practices, cacti are good for warding off intruders and what are Alien Parasites if not intruders? The spines are said to catch negative energy. Cacti are one of classic Feng Shui cures used for shifting the energy and attracting wealth. However, place cacti with long and sharp spines on your window shelves to ward off negative energy from entering your house. Use a cactus, such as the San Pedro cactus with very short and few spines in other areas.

FOURTEEN: INDIGENOUS RITUALS

Take part in an indigenous North American Sweat-Lodge or an indigenous Mexican *Temazcal*. A Temazcal is a vapor bath employed in traditional Mexican healing ceremonies. Temazcal means "house of heat" in the Aztec language *Nahuatl*. It was employed by the Aztec and Olmec indigenous peoples and is still practiced today. The Sweat-Lodge is practiced by the Navajo and Sioux indigenous nations of North America.

Unlike the Sweat-Lodge, the Temazcal is usually a permanent structure. It is usually constructed from volcanic rock and cement and has a circular dome, although rectangular ones have been found at certain archeological sites. To produce the heat, volcanic stones are heated. Volcanic stones are safe because they do not explode from the temperature. They are then placed in a pit located in the center or near a wall of the Temazcal.

Traditional healing methods and rituals are performed during the Temazcal to encourage reflection and introspection. It is furthermore utilized for all matters relating to women's conditions such as: menstruation, fertility issues, the gestation period and labor. Many people today participate in a Temazcal a day before taking part in an Ayahuasca ceremony in order to remove all toxins from the body.

FIFTEEN: CORRECT YOUR MISTAKES

Correct your mistakes as much as possible. Always keep your word. If you say you are going to buy milk on your way home from work, you must do so. From the most miniscule to the grandest of tasks, if you say that you are going to do this specific chore, you must do it! The simplest decision you make; you must follow through on your decision. If you make an error in your spelling, correct it.

Also, clean your home. Do not let error creep into your home in the form of confusion and clutter. If your home is a disaster, you must organize and clean your home.

If you have lied or made a mistake, admit your lie, or mistake, and apologize. This also applies to exaggeration. Some individuals are prone to exaggeration: exaggerating their income, the size of the fish they caught, the number of homeruns they hit playing Little League baseball as children, their social status, statistics and so forth. All people have unmet needs and goals they would like to achieve in life. Therefore, people tell stories to show their bravery, to show their intelligence, all in an attempt to prove their social desirability, trying to convince others to believe their point of view. Often people who exaggerate desperately crave attention.

Don Miguel Ruiz reminds us:

Be impeccable with your word. Speak with integrity. Say only what you mean. Avoid using the word to speak against yourself or to gossip about others. Use the power of your word in the direction of truth and love.

WARNING: It is not recommended to admit to a lie just to relieve yourself from your guilt in telling a lie. Hurting another person's feelings just to relieve your guilt is despicable, and not a valid reason to be honest. The reason to admit to a lie is because of your commitment to the truth. You do not need to fill your life with untruths. Deceits, exaggerations, lies, slanders, inaccuracies and libels, open you up to Archontic assault and control.

Have courage to admit your untruths. Then, wonderfully, you will feel a very real and authentic sense of your bravery and worth, for the reason that you are doing something truly courageous. It may seem counterintuitive, but by admitting to saying or writing a falsehood, distortion, or misrepresentation, you will feel better about yourself.

SIXTEEN: UNLIMITED IMAGINATION

Unmask evil by revealing its roots. The divine human imagination is the source of all reality. In fact, all battles are fought on the field of imagination. Albert Einstein pronounced:

Imagination is more important than knowledge. Knowledge is limited. Imagination encircles the world.

Through humanity's innate creativity, worlds upon worlds are created. Every day one passes through innumerable worlds. This idea may seem strange at first, but consider how often you can change a day that appears to be a total disaster to a day that is rewarding, simply by changing how you are imagining the day. Human beings love to label things and days are no different. If you experience a series of unpleasant events on your daily commute to work, you frequently declare, "*This day is awful. I must have woken up on the wrong side of the bed this morning.*" And through these prophetic words, you have just created the day you are now living. Everything will go wrong; just as you prophesized.

Imagine you are having an argument with your sweetheart or spouse. You are angry and you begin to wonder if maybe you should break off the relationship or end the marriage. Maybe you go for a walk by yourself to a chapel or wooded area to pray and seek guidance. Suddenly, you feel your heart break in a sudden rush of compassion for your loved one. You wonder why you were even fighting. You cannot remember the reason, or if you do, everything suddenly falls into perspective, and you realize that the issue really amounted to very little when viewed from the all-encompassing perspective of all the beautiful things that your loved one has done for you. What happened? Your walk, the appearance of the chapel or forest, changed your world. Truly, you entered another universe. People say things like, "I snapped out of it!" What did they snap out of? They snapped out of a hypnotic trance. They were living in their imaginative world. Daydreaming, if you will. Their imagination had taken control of them and had begun to take them into a kind of hell.

Your imagination is more powerful than you can possibly imagine. Thus, you need to guard it carefully, and not allow it to "run on automatic." A human being's subconscious mind, out of its innate creative ability, will automatically join together similar emotions, images and thoughts. When used for creative projects, this is a very useful human ability. However, picturing your worse fears coming true, is a misuse of your faculty of imagination. William Blake tells us:

Eternity Exists and All things in Eternity Independent of Creation which was an act of Mercy. By this it will be seen that I do not consider either the Just or the Wicked to be in a Supreme State but to be every one of them States of the Sleep which the Soul may fall into in its Deadly Dreams of Good and Evil when it leaves Paradise following the Serpent.

Neville Goddard, a remarkable "New Thought" advocate of unusually keen foresight shared the following with his audience:

Now, until you are born from above, you operate the power which gives life to this world. For the world is a dream filled with dead scenery, while you are Proteus. As you enter the scene you cause the parts to be made alive. Not knowing this, you think there are others, and fight the shadows of your own being.

It is advisable to interrupt undesirable images that appear in your mind's eye. You can do this by clapping your hands, singing a favorite song, moving yourself physically to another location, rearranging your furniture or decorations in your home, snapping a rubber band around your wrist, shouting "Stop," doing 10 pushups and the like.

Sometimes, you will find yourself in a situation in which you need to interrupt the mind pattern of another person. If someone is attempting to start an argument with you, instead of responding with a counterargument or a string of expletives, perhaps bend down and begin tying your shoes. Or you may offer the other person a piece of gum. You can begin to ask about a building near you and point to it. Then point to the newspaper in your hand and say forcefully, "Have you seen this?" At this moment, you have broken the negative imaginative vision of the other person, and so seize the opportunity and suggest that the two of you will agree to meet tomorrow and have an enjoyable time together discussing the subject at hand.

Miguel Conner's great quote,

Write your own gospel and live your own myth. In other words, be the author of your own fan fiction, instead of the marketing, political and religious ghost writers hired by wickedness in high places,

now begins to reveal its full depth and meaning.

Many a person exploring Gnosticism at first will choose the "school" of Gnosticism with which that person resonates the most. The author has not discussed this in excessive detail, however, there can be great differences in the various approaches of the various Gnostic schools both from the time of Christ Jesus up until the present day. The various schools of Gnosticism, such as: Sethian-Barbeloite, Simonian, Valentinian, Basilideans, Marcion, Naassenes, Ophites, Carpocratians, Manichaeism, Mandaeanism, are very similar to all the various denominations of Christianity, in that they often have a great deal in common, and at the same time disagree strongly about other matters. It is recommended that the beginner first read a complete translation of all the Nag Hammadi codices. Familiarize yourself with the texts themselves. Do not permit anyone to tell you that you need him or her to point out which specific parts of which specific books you need to read. Remember all this is about your personal spiritual development; not some expert's opinion on how you should go about exploring your spirituality.

Do not cling to the shore, but set sail for exotic lands and places not found on maps. Walk on hallowed grounds. Blaze new trails. The term "synchronicity" was coined in the 1950s by the Swiss psychologist Carl Jung, to describe uncanny coincidences that seem to be meaningful. The Greek roots are *syn-*, "together," and *khronos*, "time." Synchronicity is the effector of Gnosis. Explore the Bogomils and the Cathars not just through books but, if at all possible, by visiting their lands, cemeteries and descendants. Finally, explore the most contemporary manifestations of Gnosticism: the writings of C.G. Jung, Jorge Luis Borges, Aleister Crowley, René Guénon, Hermann Hesse, Philip K. Dick, and Albert Camus. Delve into the many films and series that have Gnostic themes such as: Blade Runner, The Matrix Trilogy, Mother!, Groundhog Day, Snowpiercer, Angel Heart, Inception, Jacob's Ladder, Blade Runner 2049, Eternal Sunshine of the Spotless Mind, The Fountain, Cloud Atlas, The Thirteenth Floor, Jupiter Ascending, eXistenZ, Donnie Darko, Coherence, Naked Lunch, They Live, Dark City, The Truman Show, The X-Files, The Twilight Zone, Star Trek,

The Prisoner, Westworld, Twin Peaks, Fringe, The Nines, Lucy and Pleasantville. Gradually, you will begin to understand the various thought currents and systems existing in Gnosticism, and you will have begun to understand what does and does not appeal to you in Gnostic thought.

It is through your imagination that you begin to write your gospel and to create your myth. Your imagination is holy. Human beings with imagination wrote all the holy books the world has ever known. Still, your imagination can be invaded by Archons who will trick your imagination into creating all sorts of hells.

Thus, the greatest of all the techniques given here in this book, is the recommended task given by Miguel Conner:

Write your own gospel and live your own myth...or someone else will do that for you.

It is time to stop bowing down to other people's gods, obeying catechism rules written by old, celibate men and spending your life studying the holy books that (in reality) were only considered holy by the men who wrote them and then they forced and convinced, in one way or another, others to believe that these were "revealed" scriptures. Who is the authority that decides what writings are "revealed" and which are not? You are your own prophet. The experts in the field of Gnostic studies are not so well informed about the practical and ritual side of Gnosticism as they are about its doctrinal and theoretical side. Probably, some of you will complete a selection of books by Gnostics or about Gnosticism, and say to yourself, "Well, this is all wonderful and magnificent, but tell me what to do!" This is where the profound advice of the modern Gnostic, Miguel Conner, comes into play.

His advice is not some kind of "free pass" to go out and do what you want. Your task is, in actual fact, to write your own gospel and live your own myth. Some individuals actually take pen in hand, because handwriting is always more spiritually potent than typing on a word processor, and physically write out on paper their gospel. Remember: you are free to re-write your own gospel as many times as you wish. Your mythology can and will change as you grow older and you learn more about life and the spiritual worlds. You are free to abrogate as many verses of your gospel as you wish, and even to be your own heretic.

Here is the beginning of integrity. A human being who deeply looks into himself or herself and asks: Who am I? What is the meaning of life? Why am I here? Why is anything here? What is real? What happens after I die? What is actually worth doing? and so forth, begins to find within himself or herself their authentic beliefs. It is helpful in this effort to experiment with automatic writing, in order that you may allow your subconscious mind to tell you truths that you have stored in the basement of your mind.

Many individuals are living other people's lives. Consciously, you may believe you are a wonderfully spiritual, good and kind person. In reality, perhaps, you are just wearing a *persona* designed to deflect attention away from the fact that you are a manipulative, fearful, angry person, who craves fame and attention. What is a *persona*? A *persona* is the role that one assumes or displays in public or society, and also defined as a personal façade that one present to the world. The last thing the person wearing the mask wants to do is to take off the mask. Therefore, beware while you are writing your gospel and living your myth, that they are truly yours and not the *persona* with which you disguise yourself when you are interacting with other people.

In this regard, other modalities can be very helpful to bypass the falsities of your *persona* and masks that you wear. Simply put, you explore entheogens, DMT as well as other consciousness altering techniques such as ecstasy breathing, isolation tanks, rebirthing, shamanic drumming, vision quests and so on, in order to transcend the deceptiveness of your conscious mind. One of the most effective methods, and inexpensive, is dream work. Dreams will reveal all your secrets to you and to you alone. You will need to keep a dream journal by your bed and a bed light and pen to write down your dreams. At first, this process can be uncomfortable, as everyone wants to sleep peacefully and not have to wake up in the middle of the night to write down their dreams. But the riches you will discover in your dreams are worth more than all the gold in the world. Unfortunately, while many of the above techniques may take time, effort and maybe some money, this step is absolutely necessary. For Archons are constantly whispering into human ears all sorts of lies. They can make you believe you are Jesus, the Savior of the World, Elijah, a reincarnation of Nefertiti and the list goes on and on. They can also make you believe that you are a worthless piece of nothing that does not deserve to live on this Earth and that you should end your life all now. Therefore, you must first create a sacred space, using any of the many techniques given in this book and second, put your conscious mind aside for a while in order to contact your subconscious.

Thus, you will come to know your deepest desires, hopes and fears. You may be surprised to learn that some of your greatest fears are not that you are crazy or a would-be serial killer, but that you want to be a poet. Far too many times a young boy is brought up by a brutal violent father who cannot conceive of his son ever becoming something like a poet. Perhaps the boy was caught once writing a poem, and his father severely beat him to within an inch of his life! That boy then grew up to be a man who completely repressed all thoughts of writing poetry, and instead became a violent and cruel soldier. The last thing this person would want to encounter in his dreams was that he loves poetry. The maxim

"Know thyself," can be a sharp and painful sword, but it must be endured in order to be a True Human Being. When you begin to know the true You, then you can begin to write your own Gospel and live your own Myth.

SEVENTEEN: SOLAR BREATHING

Work with your breath. Many folks breathe very shallowly. To successfully accomplish this technique, you will need to breathe very deeply for an extended period of time. One of the benefits of this technique is that you will fill your body with *orgone* energy. Wilhelm Reich coined the term *Orgone* to describe the essential energy of life everywhere throughout nature. *Orgone* is the universal Life force, the basic building block of all organic and inorganic matter on the material planet. *Orgone* is also known as *prana*, life force, the fifth element, *ki, chi, élan vital, mana* and universal energy.

The second benefit of this breathing technique will be an alteration in your consciousness. You will not only be able to see orgone in the sky, but you will be able to actually view the interior of your body, as if you were viewing a CT Scan (a computed tomography scan) live and in full color. The benefits of this breathing technique are extensive. You skin and overall appearance will take on a much more youthful look. Your posture will improve. You will free yourself from emotional rigidity and inhibition. Most importantly, perhaps, is that you will super-oxygenate your brain, helping you to think more clearly and deeply.

You may practice the following technique while standing or lying down flat on your back. Take a deep breath by first filling your belly with air, and then your chest with air. A large majority of people never move their chests when they inhale. This is due to an emotional/physical response to trauma in their childhood. Watch a newborn baby breathe, and see how his or her entire torso inflates when he or she breathes. This is called solar respiration. Breathe with your mouth open, open up your jaw as wide open as possible. You will know that you are breathing correctly when you hear the inrushing and outrushing breath sounding very clearly. This sound is like the ocean you hear when you place your ear against a seashell. This is the same breath sound you make after running a race, or while having sex. Do not be disturbed if you feel dizzy. Simply place your attention on the soles of your feet and continue to breathe - if you do this, you will stop feeling dizzy. Do this practice every day, gradually working up to twenty minutes per day of continuous solar breathing. If possible, do this practice outside in nature, standing with your knees very slightly bent (not locked) and in your bare feet, on the soil, grass, or natural rock.

Whilhelm Reich wrote,

Once we open up to the flow of energy within our body, we can also open up to the flow of energy in the universe.

EIGHTEEN: ACADEMIA, SCHOLARS and SCIENTISM

Academic and scholarly study are absolutely necessary for humanity's continued understanding of itself and the world around it. However, a sense of inhumanity has begun to creep over science and academia, a kind of bureaucracy that chokes almost all possibility of real discovery from ever happening, and even worse, a belief system that very meticulously and deliberately attacks spirituality, religion and consciousness in every way possible. Materialist science reduces everything to matter. The human being, in the opinion of the materialist scientist, is nothing more than meat.

Examples of statements made by famous scientists that reveal their hidden agenda:

The Cosmos is all that is or ever was or ever will be.

Carl Sagan, Cosmos

The more the universe seems comprehensible, the more it also seems pointless.

Stephen Weinburg, The First Three Minutes

We can be proud as a species because, having discovered that we are alone, we owe the gods very little.

E. O. Wilson, Consilience

First, a definition of terms will be helpful here. Who or what is an academic? An academic is a member of an academy, college, or university; an academician. An academic is someone who conforms to a set of rules and traditions; conventional; formalistic. The academic is usually a scholarly person. Second, people who conform to a scientific or academic world view generally hold that certain areas of study are inappropriate areas of scientific research; some of these forbidden areas of exploration are: Acupuncture, Applied kinesiology, Ancient astronauts, Body memory, Chiropractic, Cryonics, Electromagnetic hypersensitivity, 366 geometry or Megalithic geometry, Naturopathy, Reincarnation, Reiki, Traditional Chinese Medicine, Graphology, Myers–Briggs Type Indicator, Neuro-linguistic programming, Parapsychology, Psychoanalysis, Phantom time hypothesis, Fomenko's chronology, Morphic Resonance, Torsion field, among many others.

Consciousness is the greatest mystery of science. Scientists know that consciousness has something to do with the brain, but scientists do not know how the brain produces consciousness. Scientists call consciousness the "hard problem." In spite of all this, progressively more individuals assert that knowledge about reality comes solely from science. It is a belief system in materialist science that is spreading across the world. This belief system does not realize it is, in reality, a religion. In brief, this new belief system is what is known as "Scientism." Scientism is nothing less than a wolf in sheep's clothing. It is the Demiurge masquerading as reasonable academic inquiry.

The worldview of science today is that human beings are nothing but robots with brains that are nothing more than genetically controlled bio-computers. The Scientism Dogma states that humans do not have consciousness, and that consciousness is nothing more than physical states acting in the brain. This is sadly the default world view of educated people. Dreams are said by scientists to be nothing more than the "garbage dump" of the brain that takes place every night.

Biologists can continue to perform autopsies, and obtain valuable information about the functioning of the human body, but never will an autopsy reveal what makes a pile of flesh, bones and blood into a human being.

As John Haught observes:

But if faith in God requires independent scientific confirmation, what about the colossal faith our new atheists place in science itself? Exactly what are the independent scientific experiments, we might ask, that could provide "evidence" for the hypothesis that all true knowledge must be based on the paradigm of scientific inquiry? If faith requires independent confirmation, what is the independent (nonfaith) method of demonstrating that their own faith in the all-encompassing cognitional scope of science is reasonable? If science itself is the only way to provide such independent assessment, then the quest for proper validation only moves the justification process in the direction of an infinite regress.

Unfortunately, many scientists have lost sight of the fact that science is based on a faith that there exist rational, discoverable laws. Indeed, scientists have their own faith. For example, one of Scientism's dogma is that all of reality came to being from nothing, and then this nothing exploded and created all of reality. A more fantastical and fable-like story could not be imagined! Science cannot explain the origin of consciousness, and the origin of the fundamental laws of the universe, among many other aspects of the universe. Science has invented what they call "Dark Matter/Energy," and they tell the general public that up to 95% of the universe is made up of Dark Matter and Dark Energy, yet scientists do not have the slightest idea of what Dark Matter and Dark Energy are.

Countless scientists (most definitely not all) forget that the crux of science is the exploration of the world and making new discoveries. However, today's science has narrowed the extent and class of discoveries that can be made. A specific quantum particle, for example, may be the subject for a search. Science has set up fences around many areas of study, with very large "Stay Out!" signs placed in possible areas of inquiry, to prevent any open-minded researcher who wants to explore these prohibited areas from daring to enter and thereby destroying his or her career in academia. Many a young scientist has lost his or her research funding because he or she began to explore forbidden areas of inquiry. This is how Scientism has created its ow proper dogma.

For example, it is prohibited to discuss the possibility that an *advanced* human civilization existed on this earth, more than 15,000 years ago. It is prohibited to date the Pyramids of Giza and the Sphinx to before the Egyptian civilization. It is prohibited to do experimental research into extrasensory perception (supersensible perception). It is prohibited to explore alternative methods of healing that are not based on mechanical/chemical laws.

This author was taught in grammar school that human civilization only went back a few thousand years, before the common era, to the time of the Mesopotamian civilizations. Now, discoveries in Turkey, such as Göbekli Tepe (a sophisticated temple complex), have dated human civilization back to 12,000 BCE. Göbekli Tepe predates the era of Sumer, considered one of the earliest true civilizations, and the invention of writing, by 6,000 years! Also, this author was taught about the atom in school, and how the electron was like a tiny planet orbiting around a nucleus of protons and neutrons. No one today believes that this Rutherford–Bohr model of the atom accurately portrays the atom.

Science has and continues to make huge mistakes, and yet continues to arrogantly declare itself as the end all and be all of rational explanation of the universe. What are some of sciences big gaffs? The list is almost endless: the efficacy of frontal lobotomies, The Blank Slate theory (*or Tabula rasa*), Phlogiston Theory, the definition of the "GENE" (which has changed over and over since it was coined by Johansson in 1909), that information cannot be sent faster than the speed of light, classifying humans into the different races, the invention of nuclear weapons, fossil fuels, CFCs (chlorofluorocarbons), leaded petrol and DDT. Examples of the errors of academia and science are presented in the magazine *The Economist*.

A rule of thumb among biotechnology venture-capitalists is that half of published research cannot be replicated. Even that may be optimistic. Last year researchers at one biotech firm, Amgen, found they could reproduce just six of 53 "landmark" studies in cancer research. Earlier, a group at Bayer, a drug company, managed to repeat just a quarter of 67 similarly important papers. A leading computer scientist frets that three-quarters of papers in his subfield are bunk. In 2000-10 roughly 80,000 patients took part in clinical trials based on research that was later retracted because of mistakes or improprieties.

Open-minded scientists of the past were regularly subjected to all sorts of abuse. For example, Alfred Wegener, was the individual who suggested "continental drift," and formulated the idea that a supercontinent known as Pangaea existed on the Earth millions of years ago. His ideas were largely ignored at the time, and he was subjected to terribly harsh criticism, while today his theories are considered absolutely solid scientific thought. By the time of his death in 1930, his ideas were almost entirely rejected by the scientific community. However, today, few scientists dare to explore and do ground-breaking research, for fear of the terrible backlash of the scientific community, and their great variety of methods for destroying the careers of scientists who are pushing the boundaries of the known world.

There is nothing inherently scientific about materialism. Materialism is a cultural affectation. Physicist Eugene Wigner penned in *Symmetries and Reflections: Scientific Essays:*

[while a number of philosophical ideas] may be logically consistent with present quantum mechanics, . . .materialism is not.

In reality, science has a profound connection to religion, and religion has a profound connection to science. For example, in *Anthroposophy* (also called Spiritual Science), meaning the study of the human being, developed by Rudolf Steiner Ph.D., an enormous significance is placed on the scientific study of spirituality. Steiner taught methods that could be tested and retested using the scientific method. He did not believe science and spirituality were mutually exclusive, but rather could actually work together. Dr. Steiner saw science as only one way of viewing the cosmos. Like a diamond with many facets, he saw reality as multi-faceted, and therefore approachable via many pathways. Anthroposophy can be defined as the Cosmic Wisdom of the Christos. It also may be defined as a merger of the words "Human" which in this sense represents the "Christos," and "Sophia" - - - therefore, *AnthropoSophia* signifies the syzygy: ChristoSophia.

Stephan A. Schwartz, a Distinguished Consulting Faculty Member of Saybrook University, a Fellow of the William James Center for Consciousness Studies, Sofia University and a Research Associate of the Cognitive Sciences Laboratory of the Laboratories for Fundamental Research, has some remarkable insights into the subject of science and spirituality. He reveals that rituals are essentially protocols, and protocols are essentially rituals. Both require focus and intent. Always there is a place required: for example, an Isolated Etruscan Oak Grove or a Scientific Particle

Collider Laboratory. Both places are places of intentioned focused awareness. Intentioned focused awareness creates a kind of sacred space. Stephan A. Schwartz continues his explanation as summarized: in various religious and spiritual groups, people first make a statement (or recitation) of collective intention: a creed, a special prayer, an opening ritual that is repeated every time the group meets. This prayer or action results in a synchronization of the conscious minds of all the participants. Totems like rosaries, religious statues and structured prayers help the follower to develop intentioned focused awareness, which research has shown is the key to opening to nonlocal awareness.

Schwartz resumes:

Through all of the rituals there are prayers, sermons and homilies, all oriented toward creating common intention, and this is accompanied by singing, chanting, dancing, drumming to further augment this linkage. Brain entraining ensues in which the congregation's brains become synched.

A place that is the site of intentioned focused awareness gradually becomes a sacred space, or in science one will say that it is a target that has a high level of numinosity. Numinosity, as Schwartz defines the word comes from the writings of C.G. Jung. Jung disclosed that:

We should not be in the least surprised if the empirical manifestations of unconscious contents bear all the marks of some-thing illimitable, something not determined by space time. This quality is numinous.... numina are psychic entia...

Jung says, "numina are psychic entia." What are entia?

Entia signifies existing or real things; in other words, entities. Psychic entia exist beyond time and space. Schwartz further observes:

Numina, I believe, should be thought of as information. Numinosity is a kind of nonlocal informational architecture that can be detected by consciousness, and to some degree manipulated through intentioned focused awareness. The more frequently attention is focused on anything the more it develops numinous qualities, which may be of positive or negative valence. The more numinous the object, the easier it becomes for others to unconsciously sense this quality. Numinous constructs excite a stronger psychophysical response than mundane objects, and as such they can be unconsciously discriminated from less-numinous objects.

British physicist-theologian John Polkinghorne has observed:

The first order experience of the scientific community strongly encourages the sense of discovery.

Therefore, in the opinion of this author, the great danger of Scientism is that this worldview vociferously denies the existence of God or the soul. Atheism is a mandatory prerequisite for participating in this worldview with other adherents of Scientism. For these people, things such as souls are not items of knowledge; they are only items of belief. Their disdain, contempt and derision for anyone who believes in the Divine is truly remarkable. In general, the arrogant outlook of Scientism causes increasingly more people to reject all forms of spirituality as delusional and lacking in any true rationality. In their opinion, the spiritual world is pure fantasy, and spiritual powers cannot be proved true. This opens the door, wide open, to the Archontic powers who want to destroy all trace of spirituality and place mechanistic and materialistic world views on pedestals. A war on consciousness is taking place in the world today, and the rationale for this war is supplied by governments, scientists and pharmaceutical companies. Governments prohibit the ingesting of entheogens (plant allies) that help people evolve their spiritual senses so that they can become aware of the Archons, the Pleroma, Gaia-Sophia and the Christos, in short so that people can become aware of:

more than human realms of consciousness

as Rupert Sheldrake explained during an interview on the internet channel *Rebel Wisdom* interview entitled, "Rupert Sheldrake: The Death of New Atheism?"

Humanity desperately needs a reconnection to Spirit. There are now increasingly more scientists who are exploring consciousness expansion, which includes the ingestion of entheogens such as ayahuasca, as well as non-chemical ways (meditation for example) to develop spiritual awareness. Humanity needs a greater say about how they choose to make this reconnection with the Divine. Every human being needs a greater sense of meaning, validation and empowerment in his or her life.

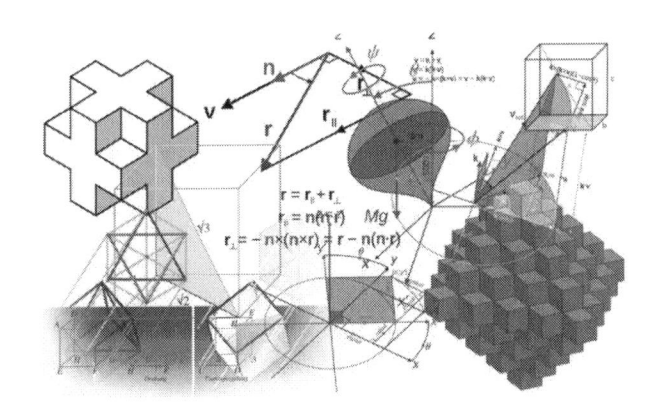

NINETEEN: AVOID NEGATIVE INFORMATION

Stay away from cable news, polemical magazines, tabloids, cynical videos (including supposedly funny videos of people being hurt) and newspapers filled with negative messages and horrible pictures. Alien Parasites enter your mind when you read and see this kind of malignant information. Here you are faced with a dilemma. Many individuals want to be informed about the world around them. However, it is easy to be manipulated into believing that you need to be familiar with all the information about which the news services tell you that you must know. You have a responsibility to prioritize your life. This responsibility is ultimately to yourself alone. That is to say, once you have decided on your goals in life, you are only sabotaging yourself if you spend your time involved in activities that will not lead you to your goals. The Alien Parasites want to distract you as much as possible from anything having to do with spirituality. In this book you are learning about the subtle tactics of the Alien Parasites and how to prevent them from possessing you, as well as how to remove them if you are already in the grip of demonic alien forces.

Every archetypical town needs individuals who specialize in various areas, in order to be a well-functioning town. The town needs a blacksmith, scribe, minstrel, stonemason, miller, falconer, butcher, grocer, baker, plowman, armorer, carpenter, among other occupations. In today's ever-increasing world of complexity, it is impossible to know everything about everything. Even in a given field, there is so much data and specialization, that for example a mathematician cannot read all the journals and magazines about mathematics. This feat is simply impossible; one cannot keep up with all the new findings in every aspect of mathematics. In today's world, people must specialize in very narrow "slices" of a particular field of study. The point of all this is that it is silly if you imagine you can truly explore, in a profound way, a field such as Gnosticism and simultaneously be an expert in international politics, nutrition, body building and so forth. Yes, there are many people who know some information a vast number of subjects. It is true that some people have doctorates in multiple disciplines, but even in these cases, these people must sacrifice great parts of their lives in order to accomplish this feat. For example, they must forego socializing with friends, taking vacations, spending time with their children, and trading off many other pleasures.

Ask yourself if it is truly your duty to explore all the day's news about your favorite political party, decide on how you stand regarding the latest war, listen to weather forecasts in other continents, and look at photos of yesterday's auto crashes and murders? Increasingly, you have less and less time. Social media constantly is calling out to you to pay attention to it, to feed it with new posts, commenting on other people's posts and just mindlessly shifting through great quantities of useless information. You must carefully guard your mind. In this archetypical town, would the guards at the gates allow just anybody and anything to enter the town? No. The responsibility of the guards is not to allow criminals, enemies and sick people from entering the town. Likewise, it is your responsibility to prevent anything from entering your consciousness that can cause you distress, anxiety, anger, rage and fear. Too many people, through the ease of turning on their television or digital devices, are inviting Alien Parasites into their minds.

TWENTY: DANGEROUS SPIRITUAL PATHS AND SPIRITUAL LEADERS

If you are a member of a religion or a spiritual path that forces you to give up your innate sense of right and wrong, leave that group immediately! If you feel that what they are telling you to do is absurd, then run out of that building. If you feel that your pastor, priest or spiritual teacher, is pressuring you to live a life that goes against your beliefs and intuition, leave that church. Your spiritual teacher may be an ordained Jewish Rabbi, Hindu Guru, Buddhist Monk, Catholic Priest, a person with a Doctorate in Divinity or Theology, or an Ascended Master channeled through someone. Their credentials do not matter. They may have all sorts of official credentials. Your consciousness and intuition are more important than your teacher's credentials or impressive robes. If what they are teaching feels wrong to you, then you must protect yourself and immediately cease all contact with the group. Alien Parasites are very subtle and can enter through a variety of methods and avenues, even via religious and spiritual teachers. Please read the last chapter about questions that have been raised about Samael Aun Weor and groups associated with him before closing this book.

TWENTY-ONE: DEPRESSING TALK

Stop participating in depressing conversations with your friends, neighbors and strangers about how terrible the world is, how much you hate certain politicians, your boss, or your coworkers. You can make a greater change in your world if you stop complaining about everything and everyone, and instead focus on what you admire. There is an apocryphal esoteric tale about the Christos that very much applies to this situation. One day the Christos and His closest students were walking across a bridge. Spiritually, bridges represent a way to "cross over," a means to arrive at a greater truth, and a means to overcome obstacles. Bridges are an isthmus between life and death, a liminal (in-between) experience. While walking across the bridge, suddenly the Apostles rushed the Christos to one side of the bridge, indicating that they did not want Him to see something. The Christos demanded that the Apostles move out of the way and allow Him to see what they were hiding. The Christos looked down and saw that the Apostles had been hiding a dead dog that was in an advanced state of decay and putrefaction. Rather than covering His nose and turning away, instead the Christos knelt down and regarded the dog. Then he turned his gaze toward the Apostles and said, "Look at the beautiful white teeth of this dog." The Christos was teaching His Apostles that it is important to notice what is admirable and beautiful even in what most people would regard as repulsive.

You too have the option to cross over from your normal way of viewing other people and events in order to arrive at a greater truth. There is no value whatsoever in complaining and having negative conversations with others in which you talk about how terrible, difficult and hopeless the world is. Your negativity becomes a kind of infernal incense that attracts the Archons. All too often this type of negative conversation about groups of people, quickly escalates into all-out tirades filled with hate. The Archons, attracted by the aroma of negativism and nihilism, begin to whisper into these people's ears. Often, people with too much time on their hands and too much frustration and unresolved anger, begin to form in their minds the most horrific thoughts about other people. They frequently add into their thoughts something they heard in a video or mentioned by another miserable person. "Proof" is very important to these Archontic puppets, who always seem to repeat one or two stories that they believe *proves* they have a right to hate another person or group of persons. In short, to avoid Alien Parasite infestation, do not engage in the habit of gossiping or gripe sessions with other people.

TWENTY-TWO: LIGHT OF THE SPIRITUAL WORLD

Seek the Divine while you are alive! Many people never explore spirituality and religion while they are alive. They are like people who are going to take a voyage to a foreign country and do not bother to buy maps of the country, learn some words of the language spoken in this new country, obtain tourist guidebooks and ask others who have visited that country:

Please tell us about the ways and customs of this country.

When these people arrive in the foreign country without any information, they are often disoriented, confused and very vulnerable. The same experience occurs when a person, who has never explored spirituality in his life, dies. After their death, they travel to a "foreign country," in the sense that this "country" is foreign (unfamiliar) to them.

These people often feel terror and even pain after death. This terror is the source of the stories about hell. Hell is only the experience of the atheist, the uninformed, or the inexperienced when they first experience the blazing, penetrating Light of the Spiritual World. They are not accustomed to the Light and so they therefore perceive the Light as burning, blinding and painful.

However, the person who regularly practices a spiritual discipline and who has a direct relationship with the Divine, is completely at home in the Spiritual World and when this person dies, he or she is familiar with this territory and is comfortable in the beautiful Light of Divine Reality.

You need to exercise your spirituality. When you exercise your spirituality, you increase the size of your spiritual muscles and the dimensions of your spiritual consciousness. To enter the Gate of Reality you need to have peace in your heart. You cannot violently rip off the veil of the Goddess of Wisdom (the Cosmic Mother) and rape Her of Her Wisdom.

TWENTY-THREE: NEGATIVE ENERGY

Remove antiques, family heirlooms and objects from your home and place of business that are associated with painful memories. Many objects can become imbued with harmful energy and terrible things. Be very careful when purchasing second-hand items, or when moving into a new house. The negative energy contained in these objects and places can cause you to become weakened spiritually and vulnerable to an attack by Alien Parasites.

The energy that flows from the Sun is extremely powerful. The great spiritual genius Arthur Schopenhauer realized that the Sun is the physical representation of the Divine in the Solar System. Rudolf Steiner taught that the Christos at one time lived in the Sun, but traveled to the Earth to enter into the being of the Initiate Jesus at his baptism.

Therefore, if you wish to purify anything of negative energies, place it in the sunlight. The light of the sun is also helpful to keep your apartment or house free of evil influences; you can accomplish this by opening all your curtains and letting the light shine into your home. Too many people live in a self-imposed perpetual shadow world that they themselves create by always shutting their blinds, shades and curtains.

Frequently, people who are depressed (often a sign of being harrassed by Archons) hate the sunlight, hate cleanliness and despise the outdoors. If you know someone who is suffering from this kind of depression, go and visit them and, using tough love, be firm and insist that they go for a walk with you to a local park. Sunlight is a physical representation of the most powerful spiritual force in the Solar System. This book has described in detail how nature is the actual body of the Goddess Sophia. You may only be able to walk with your friend for literally only a few steps outside during the first day. However, with persistence, possibly the next day you will be able to walk to the corner. Give your friend small tasks to achieve so that they begin to feel a sense of success.

TWENTY-FOUR: INTONE DIVINE NAMES

At this point in time an ancient and very powerful secret technique will be revealed to you: Intone aloud powerful Names. Why is this a great secret? When you merely "think" a prayer in your mind, the words of the prayer continue to remain in the World of the Mind, the Mental World. When you emit tones with your voice, you incarnate the word on the material/physical plane. When you sing or say the word aloud, you are manifesting that word. As it says in the Bible:

The Word became flesh, and lived among us.

John 1:14

No longer is the word only living in the Mental Plane of thoughts, it is now vibrating with living energy in the Physical World. The Alien Parasites straddle the Spiritual and Physical Worlds because while they dwell in the Mind, they also affect your brain and your body (your actions). To combat them use the vibratory power that literally tears them apart.

Intone the Divine Names in a loud, confident voice: Sophia, Christos, Mary, Barbelo, Abraxas, and other Divine Names that you believe are sacred. [The author includes Abraxas in the sense of Epiphanius (Haer. 69, 73 f.) who designates Abraxas as "the power above all, and First Principle," "the cause and first archetype" of all things. The *Holy Book of the Great Invisible Spirit*, for instance, refers to Abrasax as an Aeon dwelling with Sophia and other Aeons of the Pleroma. Two versions of this book w found with the other Nag Hammadi codices.] Also, lift up your voice and chant the names of the Aeons such as: *Nous* (Mind), *Aletheia* (Veritas, Truth), *Zoe* (the divine life), *Norea* (Eve's daughter), *Sermo* (the Word), *Vita* (the Life), *Anthropos* (the Human Being).

Intone each Name that you have chosen at least ten times each morning before getting out of bed and before opening your eyes. Then, inhale and exhale deeply several times and open your eyes. [The Names of the Aeons vary somewhat with the different "schools" of Gnosticism. You are urged to do your own research in this matter to decide what Names you sense are filled with Divine Energy.]

There is a great need for Gnostic music, for when a person sings, he or she automatically passes into a trance state. The gift of song is one of the paramount proofs of the existence of the Absolute Reality. It is hoped that many musicians reading this will begin to compose Gnostic songs in all styles of music. Music is a direct ladder to the Pleroma, a kind of transport device (transfer bridge) into other dimensions and realms.

TWENTY-FIVE: USE AUTHENTIC ITEMS

The Alien Parasites and their evil leader Yaldabaoth are doing everything possible to create a plastic imitation of the universe. That is why truthfulness, honesty and correction of mistakes are so important in the fight against them. It is much better to decorate your home with authentic arts and crafts than to decorate your home with copies of statues and famous paintings.

The author understands that you are under pressure by the advertising and propaganda agencies to buy the most expensive decorations for your home. However, one humble and inexpensive piece of authentic artisanship is far more spiritual than a house full of expensive *imitations* of great works of art. Get rid of all synthetic furniture, fabrics, decorations and the rest. Put aside all your distractions. It is not important if you can only afford a few authentic home decorations or just a few outfits made with authentic fabrics and fibers.

Start removing objects that are nothing but lies from your life; put differently, get rid of possessions that seem to be one thing, but are another. Purge your life of furniture (made with imitation wood), and artificial fabrics (natural fabrics such as cotton and hemp are excellent). Discard imitation Persian, Turkish and indigenous American rugs. Support artisans in your home town and places that you visit, by purchasing handmade rugs and other items crafted with natural materials. In addition, many artificial fabrics and carpets that can be purchased in large department stores contain artificial fibers containing chemicals which emit fumes for many months and even years that can cause cancer, allergic reactions and worst of all, are examples of subtle intrusion tactics that the Alien Parasites use to invade your home and by means of this method invade your mind and the minds of your family.

TWENTY-SIX: ABSORB NEGATIVE ENERGIES

It should be noted that there are additional steps you can take to absorb and trap negative energy. These ancient techniques come from time-honored folk traditions around the world that have withstood the test of time. Place a glass of water under your bed every night. Be sure to discard the water in the morning. Under no circumstance drink it, give it to your pet, or water your plant with the water. Flush the water down the toilet or another drain in your home.

If you are suffering a great deal of pain during the night, also place a raw egg under your bed and be certain to dispose of it in the morning. The proper way to dispose of the egg is to throw it as far away from your home as possible. Please, be respectful of your neighbors and do not throw the egg onto their property. If you can throw it into an empty field, that is acceptable. Otherwise, hurl the egg at the nearest crossroads to your home.

Place freshly cut flowers in your home and office. You can always substitute plants with beautiful blooming flowers in place of a bouquet of flowers. When you sense you are being harassed or even assaulted by Archons in a directed and focused attack, surround your bed with a circle of salt. Sea salt is the best type of salt to protect yourself from negative energetic attacks by the Alien Parasites. Sea salt is salt that is produced by the evaporation of seawater. It is also called bay salt or solar salt. Like mined rock salt, production of sea salt has been dated to prehistoric times. In addition to placing the salt around your bed, place the salt on all the window ledges, windowsills and across the threshold to your home.

It is also necessary to physically clean your house regularly. It is said that angels will not enter a filthy home. Ask yourself: how do I enter a home? The answer is obvious...one enters by turning the doorknob. One also moves from room to room opening doors through the use of their doorknobs or other methods of moving sliding doors, and so on. Therefore, in addition to regularly sweeping your home and cleaning all surfaces, also place close attention on cleaning the front entrance doorknob to your home, as well as all mechanical means to open and close doors throughout your entire home.

There are some obvious methods that are effective, which may not as of yet dawned on you as means to prevent negative energies from entering your personal and private space.

If you have adolescents or teenagers, do not let them play with Ouija boards or have a séance. This author does not recommend the use of Ouija boards or séances for any purpose whatsoever, no matter what your age. Portals to other dimensions can be found in a variety of places, and can be opened on purpose, or by accident.

Using a Ouija board or holding a séance, is like opening your front door and allowing whatever stranger to enter into your home. You are constantly being warned to guard the information you place about yourself on social media, in order to protect yourself and your family from psychological abuse (bullying, trolls and so forth) as well as various forms of physical attack, theft, kidnapping and extortion. Therefore, do not open any dimensional portals into your soul, the souls of your family, or your physical body.

Intention is another powerful tool when it comes to blocking uninvited negative beings from entering your home. Rarely do people think about directly speaking to the spirit or entity and telling it that it does not have permission to enter (or stay) in your home. For some reason, many folks just normally assume that because an entity is disembodied, it is somehow much more powerful than them. This could not be further from the truth. Just as in a Ouija Board session, you may have a being come through who introduces herself as a woman who was a Great Temple Priestess of Aphrodite from Corinth. This sounds very impressive. However, anyone can just knock on your front door and present a business card stating that they are brain surgeon. Why do so many people so easily accept the "word" of the being coming through on the Ouija Board, and yet look askance at someone who claims to be a brain surgeon knocking at their front door?

TWENTY-SEVEN: A WHITE CANDLE

Always have a white candle burning in your home for your protection. Keep the candle in a safe place, such as your kitchen sink, bathtub, or shower, while you are asleep or away from home. It is best to purchase what are known as "7 Day Candles" that are contained in a glass container. This gives the candle greater stability should one of your animals accidentally bump into your altar or sacred space where you have lit your candle. Some people place candles on their windowsills; nevertheless, a strong sudden breeze can topple the candle, as well as a breeze that blows your curtains around which may catch fire from the candle flame. Fire is a potent source of spiritual and physical protection, but just like a hammer may help to build a house, it can also help to kill a person. Always respect fire and never take it for granted. A simple white candle can provide you with a colossal amount of protection. A white candle can also be used to replace any other color candle, as the color white includes all frequencies of the rainbow. To prove this, pass white light through a triangular glass prism. The white light becomes dispersed into a spectrum of colors. Some spiritual experts and initiates have taught that all the Gods and Goddesses are nothing more than a type of dispersion of the "white light" of the Absolute Reality. Do not neglect this easy but elegant white candle technique, for it has been known by this author to accomplish great miracles!

TWENTY-EIGHT: BE GENEROUS

What you leave behind is not what

is engraved in stone monuments,

but what is woven into the lives of others.

Pericles

Be generous. It is fear which causes you to be greedy and selfish. You know that fear attracts the parasite. When you are generous, your energy becomes so powerful that no Alien Parasite can attack you. Many men and women say great words, but the people who you remember all your life are the people who show kindness and generosity toward you when you are in need.

Generosity takes many forms. Usually people think of generosity in terms of financial charitable giving. However, you can be generous with your time, your physical energy, your knowledge, your attention and kind actions. An important point to be remembered in this regard is not to confuse generosity with charity. Generosity is unselfish giving. The generous person does not expect a favor in return for his or her act of generosity.

Generosity flows best when it flows from a compassionate heart. The Sufi "Whirling Dervish" mystics tell a story about a newcomer who just became a provisional member of the Order. When it was time for dinner, the young man was shown the way to the dining hall and told to take a seat. Upon sitting down, the novice noticed something extremely unusual. The table was set immaculately. Everything was very clean and orderly. Yet, there, in front of him, lay something he had both seen, and at the same time never seen. A certain utensil. And this certain utensil was placed neatly at each place setting. It was a spoon. But not your everyday average spoon. It was a large spoon. Yet, the young man had seen his mother serving the family using a large serving spoon, this spoon was not a serving spoon. For it was unique . . .a type of cutlery he had never seen. There was the usual oval shallow bowl of the spoon, but the handle was more than lengthy. In fact, it was so long, that he almost could reach out with the spoon and actually touch the dervish sitting across from him. The cook came out with the meal, which incidentally smelled delicious, and ladled a generous portion of stew into a bowl placed in front of everyone sitting at the table. But a terrible panic overtook the young man, as sweat began to bead on his brow and he felt a sudden sensation to run out of the room. For, he thought, "How am I going to eat my meal with a spoon three times longer (at the very least) than I have ever seen before? Everyone will laugh at me. This is obviously an evil prank they are pulling on me just because I am a newcomer. I am worthy of much better treatment than this! I have been a student of spirituality all my life, and now, this! This is too much. They are mocking me. This is no house of spirituality." And just as he thought this last thought, he began to see something quite amazing. Each dervish began to feed the dervish sitting next to him using the length of the spoon's handle to reach the other dervish! They were all feeding each other.

Throughout every person's life, after the first few years, a child learns to use utensils. Then, for the rest of the person's life, until severe illness hits or the person becomes quite aged, every person feeds themselves. People learn, bit by bit, as they grow up to take care of themselves. Society teaches the population how to fend for itself, how to go to school and receive a diploma, so that then the person can obtain a job, and to use every skill, trick and talent to obtain as much as possible of the good life.

Generally speaking, other than being taught not to break the law by abusing the rights of other individuals, people are not taught to take care of others. People usually understand the concept of caring for other people as an unpleasant burden, and they do as much as in their power to avoid taking upon themselves any such responsibility.

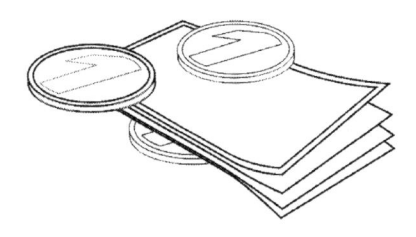

TWENTY-NINE: REORIENT YOURSELF

In the banned book *Acts of Peter*, it reads that St. Peter was crucified upside down. What is the Gnostic meaning of this strange occurrence? Gnostics see the world from an opposite viewpoint to the point of view of people who are victims of the Alien Parasites. Victims of the Archons do not see the world clearly. They live in an artificial world. In Hermes Trismegistus, *Hermetica: The Greek Corpus Hermeticum and the Latin Asclepius*, you will find many teachings that will help you to reorient yourself if the Alien Parasites are interfering with your ability to experience reality clearly. Here is one example:

"If then you do not make yourself equal to God, you cannot apprehend God; for like is known by like. Leap clear of all that is corporeal, and make yourself grown to a like expanse with that greatness which is beyond all measure; rise above all time and become eternal; then you will apprehend God. Think that for you too nothing is impossible; deem that you too are immortal, and that you are able to grasp all things in your thought, to know every craft and science; find your home in the haunts of every living creature; make yourself higher than all heights and lower than all depths; bring together in yourself all opposites of quality, heat and cold, dryness and fluidity; think that you are everywhere at once, on land, at sea, in heaven; think that you are not yet begotten, that

you are in the womb, that you are young, that you are old, that you have died, that you are in the world beyond the grave; grasp in your thought all of this at once, all times and places, all substances and qualities and magnitudes together; then you can apprehend God. But if you shut up your soul in your body, and abase yourself, and say 'I know nothing, I can do nothing; I am afraid of earth and sea, I cannot mount to heaven; I know not what I was, nor what I shall be,' then what have you to do with God? For, though, thought alone can see that which is hidden inasmuch as thought itself is hidden from sight and if even the thought which is within you is hidden from your sight, how can he, being in himself, be manifested to you through your bodily eyes? But if you have power to see with the eyes of the mind then, my son, he will manifest himself to you, for the Lord manifests himself ungrudgingly throughout all the universe and you can behold God's image with your eyes and lay hold on it with your hands."

THIRTY: ADORE THE GODDESS

Have a statue of a woman: wise, beautiful and loving to represent Sophia, and place this statue in your home in a place of honor and respect. This shall be the centerpiece of your altar to the Most Holy Goddess Sophia. Surround your altar with flowers, plants, and precious gems. Locate images (paintings, photos, sculptures) of a dove, a crescent moon and stars. Hang these on your walls or place them next to the statue. Additionally, place on your altar a chalice or cup to represent the Holy Grail and a tree (bonsai trees are excellent for this purpose) to represent the tree of knowledge of good and evil in the Garden of Eden. Burn incense: clove, eucalyptus and lemon are the best. Place a vase full of Lily of the Valley flowers near your sculpture of Sophia.

The entire process of creating an altar can take months, even years, to complete to your full satisfaction. Sophia understands if, at first, all you can afford is to draw an image of Her, or print out an image of Her from the internet, and place this on your wall. What matters most, is that you are creating a center of devotion to the Goddess Sophia, a kind of heart, in your home. You thereby show your subconscious that you are placing Sophia at the center of your life. All too often people become interested in Gnosticism, and begin to read book after book about the subject. After a while, people such as these lose interest in Gnosticism. Why? Because they never paused to reflect on the fact that they are studying a spiritual path to Gnosis. Learning about Gnosticism helps, but this learning must be put into action. If Sophia becomes nothing more to you than a principle or an example of Goddess worship in history, then She only occupies a one-dimensional place in your life. Invite the consort of the Christos into your life and home. She made the great love-leap because She loves you. Make Her real and alive in your life, and not just an intellectual concept that you find tolerable.

THIRTY-ONE: AVOID PLACES OF VICE (SLIPPERY PLACES)

Avoid visiting places where there are large amounts of people engaging in risky and unhealthy activities. For example, this book has emphasized that addictions of all types are avenues where Alien Parasites enter the minds of people. An active addict is completely in the throes of Alien Parasite infestation. The average person can inadvertently "pick up" an Alien Parasite in any location in which there are other people possessed by Alien Parasites, and those places where Alien Parasites go to look for potential new victims.

Individuals who are in recovery are always in the crosshairs of the Archons. Research shows that most define "recovery" as a commitment to being abstinent from the substance (or action) as a way of breaking its hold. Therefore, stay away from people who shared your addictive behavior and who are still engaging in it. These people (in reality often they have lost their souls – their humanity) only appear to be human. Horrifically, they are tools of powerful evil forces. These zombies are potential triggers for relapse, even if they are only related to your addiction indirectly.

In general, it is best to avoid: horse racing tracks, gambling casinos, craps, the dogs, scratch cards, slot machines, prediction markets,

Buzz Game, Foresight Exchange, Media Predict and any prediction games, games of chance, or competition on which you can place a bet that is similar. Avoid places where you can easily see people engaging in your addiction, and be extra cautious on days and events of various celebration, especially spontaneous or unexpected celebrations. It is easy to understand that if you were addicted to smoking cigarettes, that it would be a bad idea to visit some friends who are all addicted to smoking cigarettes. However, celebrations can be a more difficult and subtle situation. For example, often there is an enormous amount of emotional pressure placed on a person to attend a given event (for example the wedding of a friend). Even before the celebration, you may be pressured into buying a gift you cannot afford, and if your addiction is spending uncontrollably and compulsively, and not being able to limit your use of credit cards, you may find yourself purchasing way beyond your budget. If you are a sex addict, you may find that the wild and free atmosphere that accompanies many days of celebration, gives you too many opportunities to indulge your addiction. Or if you are a compulsive eater, normally celebrations are times when everyone overindulges in food, and as you are a food addict, just attending one celebration may cause you to fall back again into your habit of overeating.

All of humanity is under attack by the Alien Parasites that the Gnostics call the Archons. Thus, everyone needs to think "one step ahead" of the enemy. For example, if you are an alcoholic, remember that there is a reason people call alcoholic beverages "spirits." Avoid bars, especially bars with "happy hours" and "ladies drink free nights." It is of utmost importance to "know thyself." If you have never abused alcohol, then obviously it is acceptable to enjoy a few beers with your friends occasionally. However, if people who are close to you, are telling you that your personality changes when you drink, or if you notice that you are receiving more and more fines and tickets from the police for "driving while under the influence," then you must with all the fight that is left in you, seek out help. The 12-Step Programs are spiritual and have helped an enormous number of people to escape the clutches of the Archon. You often know better than other people your personal areas of weakness. If you know that every time you visit the city, you end up purchasing heroin, having sex with a prostitute, buying expensive items in high-class shops, then it is clear that you are not strong enough to visit the city. The Archons want control over you, and so any method that they can utilize to cause you to fall into a state of losing your mind, losing control, becoming mentally disorganized and completely irrational, gives them the opportunity to destroy your humanity and dignity.

Avoid groups of people who are arguing. Avoid filthy places and people who neglect their personal hygiene. Always be conscious and aware of your environment. Dance clubs that play music with lyrics that are filled with obscenities and evil ideas should be avoided. Stay away from places where people use hard drugs. A place can retain a charge of negative energy for a long time after obnoxious and electronegative people have left the location. So, do not assume that a place is safe just because evil people are not present at a particular moment. You may not physically see people present, but their negative energy signature may still be present along with the Alien Parasites which are feeding on the left-over energy in the space. Thus, throughout this book, you have been continually urged to explore methods by which you may develop your supersensible perceptions. It is always preferable to be able to know your enemy's location and attack strategies.

THIRTY-TWO: BREAK YOUR ROUTINE

Do you believe you are free of habits? Are you a machine or a human being? The answer is found in your ability to do something unique, new and original. As you observe yourself, you will become aware that humans mostly live their lives according to a regular schedule of habits. In short, they are robots. Strive to do something unusual every day. Archons cannot be spontaneous. For example, clap your hands suddenly as you read your morning newspaper or internet feed. Whatever you do, the action should be spontaneous and completely unplanned, that is, different from your usual routine. Break your habits.

If you brush your teeth with your right hand, start brushing them with your left hand. If you do not regularly donate money to homeless persons on the street, begin to do so. If you always arrange or cut your hair in a certain way, perhaps you can change your hairstyle. Listen to a music station that you do not normally play on your music system or digital device. In a conversation, make a case for the exact opposite of your usual views. Regardless, this author cannot tell you what to do, regarding breaking your usual routine, because the actions and words must be uniquely your own. These changes of habit do not need to be huge changes; the mere fact that you are doing something new has profound effects on your mind, physical body and subtle bodies.

The ultimate goal is to become a new human being. You will want to gradually change almost all aspects of your personality. As Rudolf Steiner, the renowned Christian Gnostic wrote,

We must unite ourselves and become as one with the higher truths. We must not only know them, but be able, quite as a matter of course, to manifest and administer them in living actions, even as we ordinarily eat and drink. They must become our practice, our habit, our inclination.

THIRTY-THREE: DEVELOP YOUR POTENTIAL (PART A)

It is now time to introduce you to yourself. Imagine that a doctor of Forensic Medicine performed an autopsy on a human being of great wisdom, artistic talent, scientific knowledge, in short, a polymath. What is a polymath you might ask? The word comes from the Greek: *polymathēs*, "having learned much"; and from the Latin: *homo universalis*, "universal man"). A polymath is a person whose expertise spans a significant number of subject areas, known to draw on complex bodies of knowledge to solve specific problems. Often, they have impressive memories and also are able to combine many different areas of research into bold, new approaches. However, if the doctor of Forensic Medicine should work and work for months studying the dead body of this great person, the doctor would never encounter this person. While the transhumanists want society to believe that the transhumanist scientists have mapped out the entire brain and now understand everything regarding what makes a human being a human being, the hard fact is that these scientists still do not understand consciousness. No physiological explanation exists for the human mind.

Further complicating the efforts of these scientists are new discoveries that the heart has a complex neural network that is sufficiently extensive to be characterized as a brain on the heart. The "heart-brain," as it is commonly called, or intrinsic cardiac nervous system, is an intricate network of complex ganglia, neurotransmitters, proteins and support cells. The problem does not stop there, however, as a newly discovered neural circuit directly links the brain to the human gut. Humans have a kind of sophistical neural network that is intimately involved with the bacteria in the human intestines.

Add to this amazing information that the brain extends itself far beyond the skull, and participates intimately with the heart and stomach, scientists are still working on another profound mystery. It is now well understood that the human being has what is called the "Triune Brain." Humans have an ancient brain the *Reptilian Brain* (which comes from the time when humanity's biological ancestors were reptiles), the *Mammalian Brain* (which comes from the time when humans were nothing more than animals), and the *Neo-Cortex Brain* (a very controversial part of the human brain which humanity shares with all mammals and which some claim is the part of the human brain that makes you uniquely human. Neanderthals are an extinct species or subspecies of archaic humans, with which humans interbred, and with whom humans still share part of their DNA. Recently 3 caves were discovered with artwork done by Neanderthals dated to around 65,000 years ago). However, investigators are still far from understanding why *Homo sapiens* (the scientific term for the modern human being) and its three brains makes the human being so unique.

In order to truly understand the human being, one must use the tools of supersensible wisdom – spiritual wisdom that the most highly developed spiritual sages have shared with humankind. Here, then, is a description of the human being as seen through the eyes of an Initiate:

1) Physical body is the visible and known. Gurdjieff teaches that by only rooting your consciousness in the living sensation of your body, the divine spark, your real presence, can awaken. Humans share the elements of this "physical body" in common with rocks and minerals.

Nikola Tesla (1856-1943) was the genius who lit the world, whose discoveries in the field of alternating polyphase current electricity advanced the United States and the rest of the world into the modern industrial era. He also created the "Tesla coil," which is still used in radio technology. Tesla said the following about the mineral world,

In a crystal we have the clear evidence of the existence of a formative life-principle, and though we cannot understand the life of a crystal, it is none the less a living being.

2) Etheric or Vital Body, impregnates the physical body and gives it life. The Etheric Body is the template of the physical body. It is said that it is in immediate contact with the physical body, to hold it and connect it with "higher" bodies. Humanity shares the elements of this body in common with plants and trees.

3) Astral or Desire Body, is the body of sensations, which allows the human being to feel. The body of Desire is made of desire from which human beings form feelings and emotions. People share the elements of this body in common with the animals.

4) I, or individuality, as soul nucleus, divine spark; that which makes humanity unique and different from all else. This "I" should not be confused with the "I" or the "ego" of psychology. Rudolf Steiner wrote,

The little word "I" is a name which differs from all other names. Anyone who reflects in an appropriate manner on the nature of this name, will find that in so doing an avenue to the understanding of the human being in the deeper sense is revealed. Every other name can be applied to its corresponding object by all men in the same way. Everybody can call a table "table" or a chair "chair." This is not so with the name "I." No one can use it in referring to another person; each one can call only himself "I." Never can the name "I" reach my ears from outside when it refers to me. Only from within, only through itself, can the human being refer to himself as "I."

5) The Spiritual Seity (or Transformed Astral); the same "I" acquires immortality. The word "seity" is defined by Merriam-Webster as "a quality peculiar to oneself: selfhood, individuality." The Divine Spark takes possession of the astral body by uniting itself with the secret nature of the astral body. When the astral body is overcome and transformed by the "I", it becomes the Spiritual Seity. Spiritual Seity begins only as a germ, but develops increasingly as it actively works on itself.

6) Vital Spirit, as a transformed vital body. Just as the "I" conquers the astral body by penetrating its mystical forces, so too, in the same way, the identical process can occur in the Vital Spirit or Etheric Body. One of the best means by which change occurs is through repeating an act or experiencing a spiritual feeling: for example, repeating certain religious prayers, creeds, or rituals.

7) Man-Spirit, as a transformed physical body. The work continues as the Divine Spark unites with the forces hidden in the physical body. What appears as the coarse matter of the physical body is only the *manifested* part of it. Behind this manifested part are the hidden forces of your being and these forces are of a spiritual nature. The final result is the creation of the Resurrection Body.

THIRTY-THREE: DEVELOP YOUR POTENTIAL (PART B)

Often individuals want to know why spiritual beings from a spiritual belief system, namely Gnosticism, can be called Alien or Extraterrestrial. The reason is that humanity has mistakenly thought for centuries that evil has a purely spiritual cause, and that the "devil" exists in some kind of hell where evil souls go after death. As you have just read, the human being consists of seven "bodies." Traditionally, only the Physical Body was thought to have an existence here on Planet Earth. When in reality, all the other six bodies have a direct effect on the physical body. The seven bodies all exist on various planes or dimensions. All of these planes interpenetrate one another. Many "New Age" teachers and belief systems, want people to believe that these "planes" are stacked on top of one another, and that they proceed from lower to higher vibrations.

The same notion applies to all of nature. Just because people do not see rocks walking around and talking, they assume that the mineral world is devoid of life and consciousness. Yes, the consciousness of the mineral world is evolving more gradually than that of, for instance, your pet cat. However, the consciousness of the rock is just as exalted as that of your pet, and will some day in the far distant future, evolve into an angel.

For millennia, the great spiritual Initiates have taught humanity that the Christos exists on the Etheric Plane, and only those with supersensible vision can see Him. They have imparted that the reason Mary Magdalene could "see" the Christos, is because she was one of the few in the group that possessed clairvoyant abilities. She had to gradually help the other Apostles to "see" the Christos. Error creeps in when people assume that the Etheric Plane is somehow less real than the physical plane. In point of fact, it is more real! Therefore, Alien Parasites do very much exist, on their plane and can cause immense damage to the physical and other bodies of human beings.

One of the most effective ways to strengthen the Etheric Body is to follow the exercise given above regarding learning to do everything you normally do but with the non-dominant hand. Do not just brush your teeth with your non-dominant hand, but also brush your hair, wash your body, learn to write, hold your cellphone and remotes, hold your fork and so forth, all with your non-dominant hand. This "body building" of your Etheric Body will not only make you a formidable opponent to any Alien Parasite, but will also have the added benefit of making you look younger, and will immensely improve your health.

Realize that humankind only uses a fraction of its potential. Scientists have yet to identify the purposes of large portions of human DNA. Francis Harry Compton Crick, OM, FRS, was a British physicist, molecular biologist and neuroscientist, known above all for being one of the discoverers of the molecular structure of DNA, in 1953, together with James D. Watson. He won the Nobel Prize for his discovery. Crick stated that humanity's genes were deliberately sent to Earth by extraterrestrials (beings from outer space).

Likewise, as humankind only uses a fraction of its potential, humankind only *understands* a small fraction of the universe. Your task as a student of Gnosis is to develop your unexplored capabilities. Potential requires exploration. You may be ruled and limited by illusion without realizing it. Dare to live the truth of your myth. The Alien Parasites want to keep you ignorant, asleep and intoxicated and do not want you to realize your full potential.

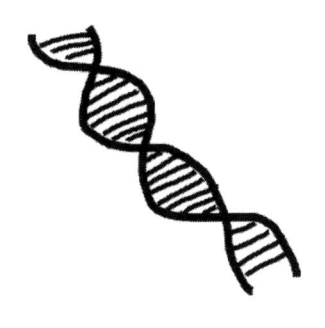

THIRTY-FOUR: REST

You should refresh yourself with seven to eight hours of sleep every night. Under no circumstances stay awake all night. Do not go out without sleep. You need to rest.

For we who have believed do enter into that rest.

Hebrews 4:3

Parasites invade a person who is tired and fatigued because his or her mind is weak and he or she is in an easily suggestible state. One of the first signs that a person is losing the battle against the Archons is when the human being enters a manic state, in other words, working non-stop on a project, without sleeping for days on end. Additionally, there is a danger in falling into the habit of oversleeping. Excessive sleep can dull your powers of concentration and awareness.

Therefore, those who are truly awake, having cast ignorance away like sleep, do not perceive the world as solid and substantial, but as a dream in the night.

Gospel of Truth

Recent scientific research is revealing that when you are in the state of dreamless sleep you are conscious! Delving more deeply into this condition uncovers a great spiritual secret. In normal everyday life, you regard objects and experiences as they relate to you. Even in dreams, experiences are happening to you. However, in deep dreamless sleep the "you" is taken out of the equation. Alva Noë, a philosopher at the University of California, Berkeley, writes,

If you take out the 'me' part, and get rid of the world and all the namable qualities like red, or hot, is there anything left over? A pure experience not of oneself, but just of being, or being alive?

In other words, this "pure experience" is the state of enlightenment. You are experiencing the world without judgement, without a 'you.' Yet, you are alert. As the Sufis say, "the drop falls into the ocean and becomes the ocean."

THIRTY-FIVE: MYSTICISM

Fear directly invites parasites to invade you. You need a direct spiritual path to the Divine. This is called the Way of the Mystic. Naturally, this book recommends the mystical path of Gnosticism.

However, other mystical paths exist that are effective if you find that Gnosticism does not resonate with your spiritual intuitions and beliefs. It is essential to realize that while religion may provide a comforting and enjoyable weekly experience, as you attend church every Sunday with your family, religion is no substitute for immediate consciousness of the ultimate reality. Religion is an organized system of beliefs, ceremonies and rules used to worship a god or a group of gods. Whereas mysticism is a transcendental union of soul or mind with the divine reality or divinity. Through mysticism one can attain immediate consciousness of the Transcendent or Ultimate Reality or God. A mystic experiences the existence of realities beyond sensory or intellectual understanding. These realities are central to being and are directly accessible by the mystic. However, do not get involved in extremist orthodox religion. Stay away from all "extremes" because extremism is the "Royal Path" to Alien Parasite possession.

WARNING: Do not fall into the error of attempting to explore more than one spiritual system at a time. This will only result in confusion and recall that confusion is an open invitation for the Alien

Parasites to take over your mind. Devote at least three years learning a spiritual system before exploring another system. Learning an enormous amount of data about a spiritual path is not at all the same as an active daily spiritual practice. Direct Knowing of the Divine will remove all fear. Obsession just leads to more agitation. Agitation leads to fear. And fear opens the door to the Mind Parasites.

To be absolutely clear: it is suggested that you practice a spiritual system of some sort. This author endorses exploring various spiritual methods until you discover which works best for you. These methods include: yoga meditation, entheogens, sensory deprivation, Wicca, fasting, sweat lodges, Advaita Vedanta, Ordo Templi Orientis, Soka Gakkai International, The Fourth Way, Arica, Zen, Neopaganism, Taoism, Anthroposophy and the like).

THIRTY-SIX: PRAYER OF ENCOURAGEMENT

The following meditation is suggested. This meditation is a form of *mantra* (continuous prayer) that you will say to the Christos. As the Buddha Dharma Education Association explains it,

Tibetans pray in a special way. They believe that when certain sounds and words, called mantras, are said many times, they arouse good vibrations within the person. If a mantra is repeated often enough it can open up the mind to a consciousness which is beyond words and thoughts.

The origin of the *Kyrie eleison* is very ancient, even pre-Christian. The invocation *Kyrie eleison* was already known in pre-Christian antiquity, specifically in pagan cults. Linguistically, the word pagan derives from the Latin word *paganus*, which means "a villager", or a "country dweller". The word pagan is frequently misunderstood and misused. The word *pagan* relates to, and is characteristic of, those people who adhere to non-Abrahamic religions, especially adherents to indigenous and earlier polytheistic beliefs. The full invocation is:

Kyrie eleison (Κύριε, ἐλέησον)

Lord, have mercy

Christe eleison (Χριστέ, ἐλέησον)

Christ, have mercy

Prayer is simultaneously a petition and a prayer of thanksgiving; an acknowledgement of what God has done; what God is doing and what God will continue to do. When you inhale, say to yourself, *Kyrie*, and when you exhale, say, *eleison*. On your next inhalation, say to yourself, *Christe* and when you exhale, *eleison*. You can continue this form of "Breath Prayer" throughout the day. If you are unsure of the pronunciation of the words, there are a multitude of videos on the Internet in which you can hear the chanting of this prayer. In like manner, if you prefer, you can use the mantra "Christos-Sophia". Inhale while saying *Christos* and exhale while saying *Sophia*. This practice helps balance the two hemispheres of the brain, reduces depression and anxiety, and increases mental coherence.

THIRTY-SEVEN: LIVE IN HARMONY

Live in harmony with the natural rhythms of the world. Honor the cycles of the moon, equinoxes and solstices. As far as possible, take nature walks - watch the skies during the day and the stars at night. Go camping alone, with friends or with family. Participate in Outdoor Festivals and Concerts. Open your curtains and let the sun into your house.

To function properly, the brain needs ultraviolet light. The incandescent light bulbs and fluorescent light bulbs in your home do not provide ultraviolent light, only the sun's rays provide ultraviolet light. Therefore, as much as possible, go outside, walk, or simply sit and enjoy the outdoors.

Ultraviolet light from the sun travels directly through the optic nerve in the eyeball into your brain. Ultraviolet light attacks and eliminates Alien Parasites. You can choose to work on a farm, join an agricultural commune or start growing a garden (where you can grow vegetables and spices). Adopt a pet. Develop your love for nature, and simultaneously you will be developing your relationship with Sophia/Gaia. Through interacting with nature, and quieting your thoughts, you will receive the "pure and immeasurable" mind, the divine mind behind nature - Sophia.

THIRTY-EIGHT: AVOID THE EXTREMES

Are you obsessed with pornography, masturbation, drugs or other toxic substances, television, gambling, the stock market, social media, the lottery, internet gadgets, bodybuilding, food, casual sex, transhumanism, clothing, shoes, cars, hedonism, jewelry, alcohol and so forth? Are you always worried, depressed, jealous, envious, angry, or violent? This book has mentioned that through these obsessions Alien Parasites find easy entrance into your mind. This is also the way Black Magicians and Evil Shamans attack you.

A psychic attack of any kind, always begins with the evil being or person looking for your "Achilles' heel." This phrase refers to a weakness in spite of overall strength, which can lead to a downfall. Almost everyone, no matter how accomplished in life, has their Achilles' heel, some weakness, some fault, that can be exploited by a black magician.

In life, you must take the "Middle Path of Moderation." "Extremes" are the paths that Alien Parasites use to enter the mind. Parasites can enter through your addictions to things or your addictions to emotions and negative thinking. Eventually, as you are overwhelmed by your addiction, you lose awareness of your direct connection to the Divine, you lose your true humanity and become nothing more than organism harboring a parasite.

THIRTY-NINE: DISTRACTION

The allures of this world are dangerous. This book has explained that Alien Parasites distract you from an awareness of your divine potential by bombarding you with an endless amount of entertainment, new things to buy and various chemical intoxicants such as alcohol and drugs. You become a happy, tranced-out consumer. However, pleasure and numbness are not their only form of attack.

Alien Parasites play a game of seesaw with you. They do this by occupying your mind with endless concerns such as: political problems in the country and the world, the bureaucracy that invades almost every aspect of your daily life, exorbitant taxes, excessive and unjust laws, corrupt politicians, fake news, disinformation, an inefficient legal system, control of the volume of cash in circulation, credit card companies that engage in usury, banks threatening to seize your car and home, repo lawyers who live off the suffering of their neighbors and compatriots, growing debt (national and personal), unjust imprisonment, government spying on its own citizens, the war on consciousness (governmental control of the individual's right to explore his or her own consciousness through the ingesting of natural entheogenic/visionary plant substances), sexual slavery, kidnapping of children, oil spills, nuclear power plant accidents, the possibility of war and being forced to fight in the war, the threat of torture or worse if you speak publicly against the government, the awareness that the military is creating super-weapons: drones, quantum computers, chimeras, "smart" goggles, weaponized animals, hummingbird drones, invisibility layers, laser rifles, "iron man" (exoskeleton suits), covertly designed biological weapons and electromagnetic pulse weapons, eugenics programs, the New World Order, the Shadow Government, and so on. Clearly, the average citizen seeks to forget all these stressful facts through partaking in sensual delights.

However, your great and heroic task is to wake up and realize that you are being treated like a puppet by the power elite. There are two types of distraction: pleasure or terror. But there exists a third point of transcendence by which you can escape from the teeter-totter between losing your mind through drugs or alcohol induced sensual intoxication orgies or losing your mind through government and military induced "orgies" of fear and panic. The third alternative is to step outside of this game of seesaw and live the life you deserve, as Gods and Goddesses on Earth.

You have a Super Potential and it is your sacred responsibility not to get lost in the maze of fear-inducing mechanisms of the power elite who are trying to control you. Remember this book has previously explained the wonderful divine-human imagination.

However, your powerful imagination can be used to confuse you! If you believe in the lies and fears of the Alien Parasites, you begin to use your divine human imagination to "out picture" (psychologically project) these lies onto your environment. Projection is the attribution of one's own attitudes, feelings, or desires to someone or something. Projection is an unconscious defense against anxiety or guilt. The Alien Parasites make you create a life, and a living environment, that mimics the same horrors that the Alien Parasites have whispered into your mind. Notwithstanding, you are astonishingly powerful! Human beings are incredibly strong when they realize their own potential. Do not base your life on your social status, but on the fulfillment of your true identity, your True Self. Forget the imaginary restraints placed upon you by the mesmerizing deceptions of the Archons.

FORTY: YOUR SACRED BODY

This last technique is necessary when you have very difficult and stubborn Alien Parasites that will not leave despite all your efforts. First, remember that Alien Parasites flourish in artificial environments. The ultimate environment, the environment that the parasite is invading, is your holy sacred body.

You might be thinking:

"What is artificial or false in my body?"

The answer is:

"Your food."

Now, this technique is only necessary if you have tried, and are actively using on a daily basis the other techniques this author has taught you. If you take a moment to think about your food, the author suspects that you will realize that you are eating and drinking foods with artificial ingredients. You are literally putting into your body foods and beverages that are full of chemicals, preservatives, hormones and other horrible "false" foods.

Read the ingredients carefully on your soft drink bottle, fruit drink, liquid yogurt and so forth. A very famous bottled breakfast drink, called "fruit", contains only 2% orange juice! The other 98% of the breakfast beverage is made with sugar and many toxic synthetic chemicals – these "synthetics" exist in your food and drink, to give them texture, color, flavor and even smell!

Since this is an "advanced technique," you may have to do a little investigating on your own. For example, many types of meat sold in supermarkets today are from animals that were fed genetically modified foods. In other words, they are no longer natural animals. Archons love to play "god" and hence they are therefore very involved with all the techniques of genetic modification that change the DNA of humans, animals, birds and plants. Farmers inject hormones into their cattle to make the cattle bigger, which makes the cows produce more milk and also for other purposes. These genetically modified foods and milk products enter your body and begin to modify your cells. This nightmare scenario happens every day in almost every farm and ranch in the world.

You should look for 100% natural, chemical-free foods that are not genetically modified and do not contain growth hormones, medications, antibiotics and other artificial substances. This technique also applies to cigarettes and alcoholic beverages. Almost every brand of cigarette contains up to fifty chemicals in every cigarette! If you must smoke cigarettes, buy chemical-free cigarettes sold by Native-Americans. Almost all brands of mixed cocktail drinks and popular "wine coolers" are filled with chemicals.

They are not made from natural and authentic ingredients. These drinks are artificial — lies in liquid form.

Addiction is the last step in the process of obtaining total control over a human being, turning the person into a Zombie. This author is not suggesting that you need to be a saintly, holier-than-thou, person who does not enjoy life. This specific technique is of great importance for those people who are plagued with very evil, powerful and stubborn Alien Parasites. The Gnostic is a person filled with joy, who enjoys all the pleasures and beauties of the glorious natural world. Nonetheless he or she is careful not to mistake the fake world of Hollywood, Las Vegas, Disneyland and television advertising propaganda, with the real authentic world.

BONUS CHAPTER: THE ARTS CAN SAVE YOUR LIFE

More wisdom can be transmitted through a novel than a textbook. Certainly, nonfiction texts and academic works can convey a huge amount of valuable data. However, the arts are closer to Wisdom than all the scholarly books that have ever been written. One of the arts is creative writing and profound secrets are hidden in novels. Cold facts never can sprout into flowers of wisdom. Rudolf Steiner called art the worthiest interpreter of the secrets of nature. There are many arts: music (instrumental and vocal), dance, drama, folk art, creative writing, architecture, painting, sculpture, photography, graphic and craft arts, industrial design, costume and fashion design, performance art, motion pictures, television, radio, film and video, to name some. Steiner says that each art presents the audience with a different 'language' that expresses certain truths living in the human soul. Therefore, not only can novels transmit great wisdom to you, but remarkable films, paintings, symphonies and operas, ballet, contemporary dance, internet radio shows and inspiring videos.

A scholarly thesis or dissertation is like an imitation seed. It will never take root in the human soul and bloom. However, a seed that comes from a plant, cactus, tree and so forth, can germinate in the soil of your soul (Sophia) and pour forth blossoms and fruits that will nourish you spiritually. Therefore, do not attempt to collect a lot of facts, in order to impress others or to obtain one degree after another. The Archons disguise facts so that they appear to be wisdom. What you need in order to strengthen yourself against all forms of Archontic attack, is living knowledge. This is Gnosis.

Living knowledge goes beyond words and lifeless facts and takes you into a wordless direct knowing of the Ultimate Reality. The spiritual forces contained in living wisdom eventually imprint themselves upon your life force and physical body, strengthening you, making you impervious to the most brutal of Archontic attacks. For the person in whose being wisdom flows, knows his or her true identity. Ultimately, all will flow back into the overarching truth of oneness. However, until that time, you must participate in the daily life that is presented to you each day.

While some individuals choose to move to remote and exotic locations and follow unique activities that provide them with a great amount of distraction from their everyday problems, there really are no short-cuts to escaping your inner pain. There is a saying, "Wherever you go; there you are." If you are filled with unresolved anger, trauma, jealousy, grief and so forth, these painful emotions will not automatically go away just because you move to Hawaii, the south of France, or take up the sport of Wingsuit flying (or wing suiting). By way of illustration, while a person living in a major city may experience road rage during their daily commute as they face thousands of other drivers on the highway, a person living in an idyllic country setting will become equally enraged if there is only *one* driver ahead of him or her on the country road, because he or she is not driving fast enough. You see, it is not your locale that makes all the difference, it is you who makes all the difference.

If you have an Archontic parasite attached to you, it will not leave without a great deal of work on your part. According to Wikipedia, in nature, the parasite uses the host's resources to fuel its life cycle. It uses the host's resources to maintain itself. Therefore, the work you must do to rid yourself of a Mind Parasite, is to stop feeding it your anger, jealousy, fear, sadness, shame, guilt and embarrassment. This takes discipline, and sometimes you must overcome your shame and embarrassment about asking someone for help, but you can successfully rid yourself of all Archons.

SECOND BONUS CHAPTER: REAL OR SPIRITUAL?

The mythologies of many of humanity's predecessors on this planet believed that their Gods and Goddesses, as well as Prophets, Avatars and so forth, were 100% real, visible and were able to cause changes in the physical earth, as well as capable of raping women, affecting crops and cattle, granting wealth to certain individuals and on and on. However, something occurred during the last 2,500 years that caused humanity to think of these beings as nothing more than "mythological characters", and the location of these beings, such as the top of a mountain, being translated as "heaven". In short, humanity's religious beliefs have become increasingly tenuous, flimsy and unsubstantial. The present day gods of humankind are invisible, and in the last 2,000 years, only made one visible appearance, Christ Jesus. But where are they now? Most adherents of these religions would reply, "in heaven." Well, where and what is "heaven"? In other words, these people are saying that all humanity's spiritual beings: angels, archangels, saints, God the Father, God the Son and God the Holy Spirit, are all invisible and living in a place that is also invisible.

All of this is a sign that materialistic science and worldviews are taking over society. Yaldabaoth wants to stamp out all traces and all possibility of free, individualized human consciousness; he wants the human not to be an individual being, but only a member of a general species of pseudo-humanity -- to be a clever, earth-bound animal, a "homunculus". The Archons are winning. Put more specifically, and more terrifyingly, the Demiurge is robbing humanity of parts of the human body. The theme of "everything eats, everything is eaten" occurred to the influential, Greek-Armenian mystic thinker G.I. Gurdjieff in the early 20th century. This concept is very ancient and can be observed through the processes of nature. The reader may have seen a comic, for example, of a small fish being eaten by a slightly larger fish, being in turn eaten by an even bigger fish and so on, ad infinitum. It can be observed that plants draw their food from the soil. The plants in turn are eaten by animals. And, for those who are not vegetarians, one can observe that for millennia, people have eaten animals. This begs this question: who eats humanity? The Demiurge and his Archons consume humanity's astral and etheric bodies. The physical body returns back to planet Earth, while a person's Spiritual Divine Spark continues to reincarnate. It is Yaldabaoth's goal to eventually imprison all of humanity permanently.

At present, the Demiurge and his group of Archons want to fill humanity with false illusions and egotism. People under the control of the Demiurge are attracted to things such as: titles, absurd ceremonies, rank, knowledge for knowledge sake and so on. Humanity must rise above the temptations of egoic titles, obsessive study and the pursuit of an endless amount of university degrees and certificates of study.

HOW TO DEFEAT THE ALIEN PARASITES

The great Initiates of the Mystery Schools taught two simple messages:

Know yourself and you will know the Universe.

and

As above, so below; as below, so above.

It is precisely in the center, whether the center is within or outside the center of the universe - the result is the same - this is where the Infinite is found. It is an error of the highest level to think that humanity is helpless against the Alien Parasites. If you choose to believe this erroneous thought, then you will know that you have misguided yourself, failed the Divine and are deliberately choosing to throw your life away. Do not give way to fear, worry and panic. You are divinely protected eternally.

Fear is possibly the easiest way for Alien Parasites to enter your mind and fully master it. You are a Son/Daughter of the Most High. You are God/Goddess, you are the infinite consciousness that is now awakening to its true reality! Gnostic study allows you to not only free yourself from fear, but also teaches you to think in a new way. For example, at the last supper, when the Christos said:

This is my body which is given for you. Do this in memory of me,

Luke 22:19

the Christos used a specific word. When He said "memory," that word meant more than *remembering an event*. The word means to *rethink or perform the event in a new way*. In other words, in the ritual of communion, Christos wants humanity to return home, to its divine origin in the Pleroma. Gnosticism is the renewal of the mind.

Maintain a firm mental attitude of courage. Let the word courage sink deep into your mind. Fear paralyzes, while courage provokes positive activity. There is real hope. Above all, do not make the mistake of thinking the world is bad. The concept that the world is bad was introduced by a Greek philosopher by the name of Bias of Priene. He is famous for saying the words:

All of the human race is wicked.

and:

Most people are evil.

These were Archontic words introduced into human society to make humans suspicious and paranoid of one another. Unquestionably, this poisonous belief became part of human nature on the outrageous instigation of the Archons before the time of Bias of Priene, however, it was this Greek philosopher who put the idea of the wickedness of humankind into the public discourse, and which thereby found its way into religious thought and belief.

The world is Christos-Sophia. Do not try to fight evil with evil. You are one with the world. Fight evil by realizing that evil is ultimately just an illusion and that the Greater Reality is You. You are the steward, and as Pascal said, *"the one immortal human"* of this planet. You are Christos-Sophia. You are One with the Pleroma. Christos-Sophia will throw the Alien Parasites out of your mind. The Archons will be erased because they never had existence or true soul. You will remember that your home is the Pleroma and that you are One with your Divine Consort. The world is an image of the Living Aeon. Its form was created by Sophia. You have forgotten your spiritual roots. You just need someone to remind you of your heavenly home. You are beginning to remember who you are and from where you came. Yet how can you travel to your heavenly home? You do not need a spaceship to fly to the center of the galaxy. Here is a great mystery: you are directly connected to the Pleroma. The entrance to your heavenly home is within you. The Christos taught humanity:

> . . . *for behold, God's Kingdom is within you.*
>
> Luke 17:21

Sri Ramana Maharshi (1879-1950) was probably the most famous sage of the twentieth century both in India and the rest of the world. Ramana Maharshi said:

Don't be fooled into imagining such a source to be some god outside of you. Your source is within yourself.

The big secret is that all of humanity has created reality. However, people need to become healed in order to remember. As Plato taught, learning is a form of remembering. The Human Being is the One Absolute Reality. Your power is infinite. Embrace immeasurable Light - Pure, Holy and Immaculate light.

THE NEXT STEP

Some Gnostics went beyond directly experiencing the divine, seeking union with the divine. This union is called *Henosis*. The objective of Henosis is the union with what is fundamental in reality: The One, The Source. This concept is developed in the *Corpus Hermeticum*. The Orthodox Church teaches something called *Theosis*. Theosis is a transforming process aimed at similarity or union with God's holiness and glorification. It is considered attainable only through a synergy (or cooperation) between human activity and God's uncreated energies (or operations). This is the new quality of consciousness that is essential to true Gnosis. The two terms, *Henosis* and *Theosis* are very similar; however, the Orthodox Church would never consider that a person can become God . . . in their opinion, he or she can only participate in the "holiness" of God, since created beings cannot become God in His transcendent essence.

However, those who practice Henosis believe that a human being can, through a certain process, attain the Divine wholeness. The culmination of Henosis is deification. The person is then dissolved, completely absorbed back into the One. The saints of the Orthodox Catholic Apostolic Church who seek Theosis are extremely humble and will never say that they seek to be equal to God. On the other hand, those who pursue Henosis must practice the deconstruction of thought, and a kind of process of emptying. Therefore, in reality, there can be no difference between Theosis and Henosis. Those who speak and write about Theosis often use terms like unification and deification. Henosis has unfortunately received a bad reputation as a teaching associated with paganism (pre-Christian beliefs) and magic (*theurgy*).

In general terms, in using the two previous definitions of Theosis and Henosis, one cannot fail to know the following. The great goal is, first, to reach Theosis (the radiant sanctity and consciousness of God), and then to practice rituals and techniques called *Theurgy* that lead to Henosis, yet stopping at the very edge of the Great Absorption, so that one retains one's unique divine fingerprint. For each person has a special, unique and real role to play in this life and your great task is to become aware of that role and, therefore, to fulfill your Divine calling, your final destiny.

CONCLUSION

Gnosticism demands your participation. Gnosticism is not a religion where you sit in the pew and a priest does all the work for you. In addition, in Gnosticism, the Godhead itself does not save you. You participate with the Divine in the continuous evolutionary process of Creation; in other words, in spiritual enlightenment. In future books, this author will reveal multilayered Gnostic techniques for spiritual development and enlightenment.

"But there is nothing covered up that will not be revealed, nor hidden that will not be known."

Luke 12:2

All these secrets will be known by the Gnostic, the person who develops a direct experience with God. The Cosmic Ear hears everything. The Eternal Mind knows all things. The human being has a direct connection to the Cosmic Ear and the Eternal Mind. And there are specific techniques, exercises and wisdom stories that will help you attain this wisdom. The patriarchal religions (Judaism, Christianity and Islam) want you to believe that you are cursed and/or defective. Christianity wants you to believe that only through Jesus can you be redeemed. However, Christians want you to feel that you do not deserve this redemption. You do not need redemption. You need to remember. You are not defective!

Western civilization is full of guilt. Guilt is the basis of most people's sense of identity. 32.5% of the world's population is Christian. If there is any sin, it is this horrible concept of guilt that patriarchal religions have instilled in the public. People walk around, living their daily lives, but feeling they lack something. On the other hand, with Gnosticism, you can know that there is a life, that this life is the Ultimate Reality and that this life is your life now! You are the incarnation of the Truth and the Living Mystery.

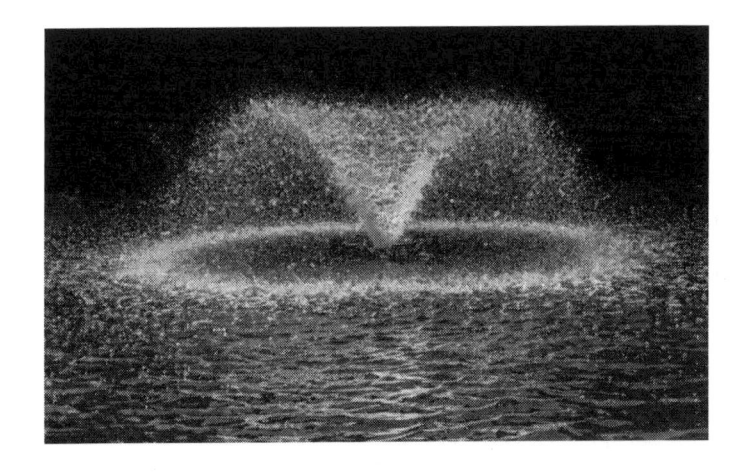

APPENDIX

Special thanks to all the exceptional contributors to this work who have generously given their permission to quote from their works:

Paul Chen, writer for THE CANADIAN, Canada's Progressive National Newspaper. B.P. 24191, 300 Eagleson Road, Kanata, Ontario K2M 2C3. Tel: (514) 712-7516, for permission to use a portion of his article "Human Oversight of Self-Awareness Reveals Manipulative Extraterrestrial Presence."

Miguel Conner, host of Aeon Byte, the only topical and guest radio show on Gnosticism, ancient mysteries and true conspiracy theories evolving since the beginning of civilization. He is author of the critically acclaimed *Voices of Gnosticism*. www.thegodabovegod.com

Jonathan Goldman is the author of *Healing Sounds: The Power of Harmonics* and The *Humming Effect: Sound Healing for Health and Happiness*, besides many music albums of his own musical compositions. Jonathan Goldman is an American author, musician and teacher in the fields of Harmonics and Sound Healing. Healing Arts Press, Rochester, Vermont.

Bubba Free John, also known as: Avatar Adi Da Samraj, as well as by many other spiritual names, was born Franklin Albert Jones (November 3, 1939 – November 27, 2008). He was an American spiritual teacher, writer and artist. He was the founder of a new religious movement known as Adidam. Bubba Free John wrote numerous books and founded his own publishing house. This book quotes from his work entitled, *Breath and Name: The Initiation and Foundation Practices of Free Spiritual Life*, San Francisco, California, The Dawn Horse Press, 1977, p. 52, 2.14.

Carl Gustav Jung, (1875-1961), was a Swiss psychiatrist and psychoanalyst who founded analytical psychology. His work has been influential in psychiatry and in the study of religion, literature and related fields. Jung was interested in the way in which symbols and common myths permeate people's thinking on both conscious and subconscious levels. This book quotes from the article of Carl Jung "On the Assumption of the Virgin Mary" – in the Anthology which in turn quotes from: *Conversations with Jung*, Page 15, and *Liber Novus*, Footnote 200, Page 299; as well as from *The Collected Works of C. G. Jung*, 8, p. 87.

John Lamb Lash, (b. 1945, New York City), has been called the true successor of Mircea Eliade and the rightful heir of Joseph Campbell. He presents a radical revision of Gnosticism, with original commentaries on the Nag Hammadi codices. He also presents the only complete restoration by any scholar of the Sophianic myth of the Pagan Mysteries, the sacred story of Gaia-

Sophia, recounting the origin of the earth and the human species from the galactic core. metahistory.org

Stephan A. Schwartz, scientist, futurist and award-winning author and novelist, columnist for EXPLORE and editor of the daily Schwartzreport.net, is a Distinguished Consulting Faculty Member of Saybrook University and Fellow of the William James Center for Consciousness Studies, Sofia University.

Henri-Charles Puech, 1978: *En quête de la gnose*, Paris, Gallimard, series "Bibliothèque des Sciences Humaines", 2 volumes Tome 1: La Gnose et le Temps.

Rebel Wisdom, a new media channel founded by BBC & Channel 4 journalist David Fuller, for their excellent show with Dr. Rupert Sheldrake, entitled: Rupert Sheldrake: The Death of New Atheism? March 12, 2019. rebelwisdom.co.uk/plans

J. Marvin Spiegelman, Ph.D. from UCLA, a Diplomate in clinical psychology, American Board of Professional Psychology. He is a graduate of the C. G. Jung Institute in Zurich, Switzerland and has taught at UCLA, USC and the Hebrew University in Jerusalem.

The World English Bible is a free updated revision of the American Standard Version. It is one of the few public domain, modern-English translations of the entire Bible, and it is freely distributed to the public using electronic formats.ebible.org/pdf/engwebp

LAURENCE GALIAN BIOGRAPHY

Laurence Galian, (b. April 5, 1954, New York City), is an internationally known author and in the words of Whitley Strieber a "brilliant and innovative researcher." Mr. Galian additionally is a professional music improviser, classical pianist, and a bearer of the title of *Seanachie* from the Temple of Danaan.

Mr. Galian studied to become a Catholic priest for several years in his youth, in the Congregation of the Passion — *Congregationis Passionis Iesu Christi* — eventually leaving the religious congregation because he wanted to have a family and continue his musical studies.

Mr. Galian maintained his search for an intimate experience with the Divine and in the ensuing years explored various esoteric traditions. Laurence studied the practices of the worship of the ancient Mother Goddess, leading him to become a Wiccan priest of the Welsh tradition, to study ecofeminism, neo-paganism and anthropology, at Hofstra University (Hempstead, New York).

In 1981, Laurence Galian met Grand Sheikh Muzaffer Ozak and was initiated as a dervish of the *Halveti-Jerrahi Order* (Istanbul, Turkey). He was also initiated into the Masters of Wisdom — *Itlak Yolu* — by Dr. Nevit Ergin. For more than twenty-five years, Mr. Galian studied and taught the Gnostic path of Sufism. Joseph Gelfer in

"Ashé Journal" writes, "Galian's task is essentially one of rediscovering lost treasure. He rediscovers the Ahlul Bayt, he rediscovers the feminine at the heart of Islam, he rediscovers the Shadow and in doing so rediscovers what it is to be a real Sufi, Muslim, and Human."

Al Anderson in *The Return of the Father of Future Ritual and Meta-Magick* calls Laurence Galian "part of a revolutionary cabal that includes Robert Anton Wilson." Mr. Galian has been a regular guest on Whitley Strieber's podcast *Dreamland*. He experienced a close encounter with two UFOs, in the presence of a witness, at Jones Beach, Long Island, New York. Laurence Galian also is an occasional guest on Miguel Conner's podcast *Aeon Byte Gnostic Radio* and Chris Snipes *The Melt*.

Laurence Galian is the recipient of a *John F. Kennedy Center* award. His original musical composition - *Zemzem* - was broadcast by National Public Radio in the United States.

Mr. Galian is the author of *Beyond Duality: The Art of Transcendence* (New Falcon Publications), *The Sun at Midnight: The Revealed Mysteries of the Ahlul Bayt Sufis* (Quiddity, Inc.) and *666: Connection with Crowley* (Amazon Kindle and Paperback). Rachel Pollack, author of *78 Degrees of Wisdom* writes "Laurence Galian has the delightful ability to take the abstruse language and dense imagery of traditional Hermetic ideas and transform them into something fresh and immediately accessible. Beyond Duality shows that Hermeticism does not have to be hidden, but can help people in living their lives."

Mr. Galian is the author of the article, "The Centrality of the Divine Feminine in Sufism," which was first published in the proceedings of the *2nd Annual Hawaii International Conference on Arts & Humanities* (Honolulu, Hawaii). The article is now featured in the anthology, *Jesus, Muhammad and the Goddess* (Amazon Kindle).

Laurence Galian is a world explorer, traveling to sites in Turkey, Azerbaijan, Bulgaria, Ireland, England, France, Canada, Colombia and continuing to probe archaeological sites in Mexico such as Xochicalco, Teotihuacan, Palenque and many others. In 2010, Laurence Galian moved to Mexico, where he currently resides, and has become a Permanent Resident.

LAURENCE GALIAN OTHER BOOKS

Beyond Duality: The Art of Transcendence (New Falcon Publications)

666: Connection with Crowley (Independently Published)

The Sun at Midnight: The Revealed Mysteries of the Ahlul Bayt Sufis (Quiddity, Inc.)

Parásitos Extraterrestres de La Mente Delirante: Como Identificarlos y Como Eliminarlos con la Espada de la Verdad Gnóstica (Amazon Digital Services LLC)

LAURENCE GALIAN WEBSITES

Laurence Galian Official Website:

quantumtheurgy.click

Facebook: (Laurence Galian Author)

www.facebook.com/ChristoSophia/

Laurence Galian YouTube Playlists:

www.youtube.com/user/Gargeniture

Laurence Galian Music:

https://tinyurl.com/yyb9674b

Amazon Author Page:

amazon.com/author/laurencegalian

Printed in France by Amazon
Brétigny-sur-Orge, FR